Rugby-Playing Man

Rugby-Playing Man

Watcyn Thomas
Foreword by Vivian Jenkins

PELHAM BOOKS

First published in Great Britain by
PELHAM BOOKS LTD
52 Bedford Square
London WC1B 3EF
1977

© *Watcyn Thomas, 1977*

ISBN 0 7207 0952 0

Printed in Great Britain by
Northumberland Press, Ltd, Gateshead
and bound by Hunter and Foulis Ltd, Edinburgh

Contents

Foreword by Vivian Jenkins   11

1. Rugby Football at Llanelli   15
2. Early Schooldays   23
3. Swansea University College   28
4. At St. Helens   39
5. International Rugby   46
6. The Bogey Slain   53
7. Wales *v.* Scotland   57
8. Waterloo Rugby Club   65
9. County Rugby with Lancashire   69
10. Wales *v.* South Africa   75
11. With the Barbarians   80
12. Lancs win the Championship   84
13. Teaching at Aston   87
14. A Poor Evacuee at Ashby de la Zouch   91
    Index   99

Illustrations

facing page

Watcyn Thomas at 21; the Llanelli XV who defeated
the Maoris in 1926   32

Wales *v.* Scotland at Cardiff in 1927   33

between pages 64-65

The Prince of Wales introduced to the Welsh team by
Watcyn Thomas

England get the ball away against Wales at
Twickenham in 1933

Watcyn Thomas scores the critical try against Scotland
at Cardiff in 1931

The victorious Welsh team who defeated England at
Twickenham in 1933

Lancashire's 14-0 win over Somerset at Bath in
June 1935   72

Watcyn Thomas is given an affectionate send-off on his
retirement from King Edward Grammar School, Aston;
reunion at London-Welsh Rugby Club   73

To the memory of my late brother and sister Cliff (steelworker) and Mabel (housewife), without whose financial help and encouragement I should not have been able to pursue my academic studies at the University College of Wales, Swansea.

My sincerest thanks to Mrs. Theresa Fowler for reading and typing my manuscript and to the *News of the World*, *Birmingham Mail* and *Birmingham Post* for their permission to include photographs.

Foreword

by Vivian Jenkins, of *The Sunday Times*

Watcyn Thomas was the Mervyn Davies of Welsh Rugby in the late twenties and early thirties. Just as 'Merv the Swerve' has become a byword among young followers of the game today, so Watcyn's name was known wherever the game was played in his own day.

Like Mervyn Davies he was a No. 8 forward, a line-out expert and a man of massive physique, around the 16 stone mark, who won fourteen Welsh caps between 1927 and 1933. Like Mervyn Davies, too, he captained Wales, most importantly of all against England at Twickenham in 1933 when Wales won there for the first time and the legend of the 'Twickenham Bogey' was broken at last.

I have good reason to remember that game because it was my own first appearance for Wales, and I can vouch for the part our captain played in bringing about our win. He was a born leader, a smiling giant who got all the fun in the world out of his rugby, but who played the game hard, in the manner of the men of the Llanelli and Swansea clubs, for both of whom he played.

In Wales, they still talk of the try he scored with a broken collar-bone against Scotland at Cardiff in 1931. Scotland were leading 8-3 at half-time, and on the re-start he was up-ended when following up the kick-off and catching the ball. He fell on his left shoulder and says 'I knew, straight away, that my collarbone had gone.' But there were no replacements in those days, so Watcyn, who was vice-captain, carried on leading the Welsh pack with his left arm clasped to his chest.

That, you might have thought, would have been enough, but later in the half he was put in possession ten yards out from the Scotland line, and promptly wrong-footed the defence before diving over the line with three Scots' defenders clinging on to him. Jack Bassett, one of Wales's greatest full-backs, converted to make it 8-all and in the last few minutes wing-three-quarter Ronnie Boon got a final try, converted by Bassett, to make it 13-8 to Wales at the close. Yet but for Watcyn Thomas's superhuman effort—merely in playing on, quite apart from scoring his try—the spoils must surely have gone to the Scots instead. That he was a truly great forward goes without saying.

A Welsh-speaking Welshman, immensely proud of the land of his birth, Watcyn has spent most of his life, ironically in a way, teaching what he calls 'basic English' to English boys in English schools. After leaving Swansea University he first taught at St. Helens, in Lancashire, and later, for many years, at King Edward's School, Aston, in Birmingham.

While in Lancashire he turned out many times for the county side, and 'Wottsyne', as they called him there—the Welsh pronunciation (Wottkinn, in phonetical terms) being too much for them!—was a great favourite in those parts. He was also a regular with the Barbarians' sides, and tales of his 'fire-worship' sessions on Easter tours (after suitable consumption of 'firewater') are still a legend in the club. Many a good shirt 'went West' in the conflagrations which were part of the rites!

Like all good Rugby men, too, Watcyn gave back to the game as much as he took out of it. For years he was an official of the English Schools' Rugby Union, and was chairman of their selectors for many seasons. 'I used to give the English XV their coaching and pep-talks before their matches,' he says, 'something which many Welshmen could not understand. But it was all done for my love of the game of rugby football. That, in the long run, is what counts most of all.'

Certainly no man, in my memory of rugby football, had more friends than Watcyn. He collected them like some Pied Piper, and was never without his band of faithful followers. His reminiscences, I'm sure, will shed new light on many aspects of the game, and add bountifully to its lore. As one of his most ardent admirers, ever since that memorable day, for us, at Twickenham in 1933, I salute him. More power to your elbow, Wat—and what an elbow!

V.J.

I   Rugby Football at Llanelli

Born and bred in Llanelli, I was nurtured in an atmosphere of rugby. It's a religion, claimed a local non-conformist preacher, who asserted in the 1920s that Llanelli had only one deity— Albert Jenkins, the local rugby hero, of whom more anon. Rugby football was the safety valve for the masses in the days of long factory hours and low wages, before the Great War of 1914-18. Up to the 1920s twelve-hour shifts were the rule in the local factories with half an hour break. Transport to the factory was by shanks' pony, there being no omnibuses, and for all this wages were minimal: £2.3s. per week for a labourer with the cost of living being comparatively high, a new suit costing £1.7s. Even in 1937, at outlying coalmines a collier's helper or Butty, working six shifts per week at the coal-face, earned only £2.2s. So it's not surprising that my first rugby 'ball' was a pig's bladder, obtained from the local abattoir and blown up by mouth.

My heritage was part of the Llanelli rugby tradition, going back to 1872, when rugby football was introduced by a young industrialist, John D. Rogers, who, appropriately, had learned the arts of the game at its birth-place, Rugby School. Rugby was suited to the Llanelli Welsh temperament, the untranslatable *'mynefferni'* attitude—'do or die'.

The club's first captain was A. Buchanan, 1875, the second being Fred Margrave in the same year. With Buckley Roderick he played for Wales in 1884. In January 1887 D. Harry Bowen played full-back for Wales against England at Stradey Park, the pitch then being situated alongside the present Furnace School. Harry Bowen won rugby immortality when, playing for Llanelli on Wednesday, December 19th, 1888, against the

Maoris (the first colonial side to visit Llanelli), he dropped a goal from near the touch-line on the half-way line, Llanelli running off winners by one dropped goal and five minors (touch downs) to five minors.

Others playing for Llanelli after this time were John Howells, later Headmaster of Park Street School; Harry Watkins, from Llandovery; and Bill Morris, the last two playing for Wales between 1896-1906. A contemporary was D. J. Daniels ('Dai Sam'), who gained eight caps between 1894-9. He was the father of 'Gipsy' Daniels, cruiser-weight champion of Great Britain in 1927, who knocked out Max Schmeling, later heavyweight champion of the world, in one round at Frankfurt.

Harry Watkins was a character. Subsequently, he was chief of the fire-brigade unit at Llandovery, one of his most notable efforts being to let a hay-rick burn out while he and his merry men had a few pints at a local inn on the way to the scene. Bill Morris, called 'Bill Cute' for his frequent asseveration that you had to be cute, went north to Rugby League. On his first night there he was saved from death by his landlady, who hearing his stertorous breathing rushed into his bedroom to find that before jumping into bed he had blown out the gas-jet, he being used to using a candle at home.

At the end of the century, the fortunes of Llanelli were at a very low ebb but in 1903 the club received a life-giving blood transfusion, when the 'Seaside Stars', a local junior club, were induced into throwing in their lot with Llanelli. Such was the interest shown in the junior side that when they played their last game before the amalgamation, against Somerset Athletic of Swansea, 5,000 spectators attended. Owen Badger of the 'Stars' became a prominent Llanelli player; he was the first of the crash-tacklers, twice breaking his collar-bone in scything down opponents. Another player was Ben Davies, great wit and raconteur. He swore the best way to catch fish was to throw an aperient into the water, and when the fish came out to relieve their feelings to hit them on the head with a mallet.

The present Stradey playing-pitch and ground was opened on October 15th, 1904. Before that the team changed at the 'Barley Mow' first, then the 'Prince of Wales' then 'The Stag', conveyance being by horse-brake. Just before the amalgamation with the 'Stars', Rhys T. Gabe joined the Llanelli club from junior club Llangennech. He played twenty-four times for Wales between 1901-8. It is interesting to speculate on how many caps he would have won in this era with its plethora of rugby international fixtures. Gabe played for Wales against New Zealand at Cardiff in 1905, when the All-Blacks lost their only game of the tour by one try to nil, the try being scored by Willie Llewellyn. New Zealand player Deans is reputed to have said on his death-bed that it was not a try, since he had grounded Llewellyn inches from the line, but Rhys Gabe told me it was a fair try.

In December 1906, Llanelli played South Africa at Stradey but lost 3-6. Tom Evans, who won twenty-two caps, scored a try. Evans helped Wales to win the Triple Crown three times between 1905-9 in the so-called Golden Era of Welsh rugby.

Llanelli won rugby immortality on October 17th, 1908, when they became the first club to defeat Australia (8-3), hence the verse in the song *Sospan Fach*, 'Who beat the Wallabies, but good old Sospan Fach'. Two prominent players in the victorious Llanelli team were Jack Auckland and A. J. Stacey. Auckland was a great wit and practical joker. Once, when *The Lighthouse Keeper's Daughter* was being performed on the stage of the local church-hall, he set a match to the 'snow' on the stage, and ruined the performance. Jack's monologues were hilarious and in great demand at the rugby-club smoking concerts. One of his best related to the cock-robin, singing a joyous song of thanks after a repast on the fresh horse-droppings of the mount of the Squire of Penllergaer, Sir W. John Llewellyn, when down came a 'Bloody great hawk' and snatched away the poor bird. The moral being that if you have a good meal, you should not make a bloody song about it. A. J. Stacey, his contemporary, became the best flat-green bowls player in the land, winning at Hastings and Llandrindod Wells many times.

Later he became an understanding and sympathetic means-test visiting officer in the 1930s, when to own a piano or even a gramophone meant no dole for a claimant.

Before the Great War, forwards like Auckland and Stacey were mere fodder-providers for the backs and dribbling was the recognised mode of progress, and when it was halted the scrum-half would whip the ball out to the backs, the ball being passed quickly to the wings. But the mode of play was changing and back row forwards were coming to the fore. In 1908-9, for example, the Swansea international back-row forward Ivor Morgan headed the list of try-scorers for his club, scoring eighteen times. He played for Wales thirteen times between 1909-12. The pattern of rugby was changing before the Great War, when the playing of club rugby was suspended.

During the First Great War the rugby game was kept alive at Llanelli by the efforts of Dick Edmunds and it was well that he did so, for in 1914 association football was making headway, Llanelli A.F.C. only just losing in the final of the Welsh F.A. Cup at Oswestry.

Dick Edmunds' XV, recruited from locals, played against Services XVs. Dick was a great character, guilty of many malapropisms and fond of using 'them big words', 'freesible' (feasible) and 'jayoparrdy' (jeopardy) being two of them. He and his team were instrumental in providing £900 for local charities, the Squire of Stradey Mr. C. W. Mansel Lewis, having granted the use of Stradey Park without charge. Llanelli R.F.C., in debt to the tune of £1,000 at Christmas 1918, had by May the following year wiped out the arrears and so successful was the club that in December 1919 it secured a renewal of the lease for another ten years.

At the resumption of club games in 1918, Llanelli had two club captains in Dick Edmunds, who was displaced by Dai Hiddlestone. They were in command of a galaxy of brilliant players who had emerged, including Edgar Morgan, Bobbie Evans, Frank Evans, H. Graham Davies, Bryn Evans and the incomparable Albert Jenkins. Dai Hiddlestone was a fitness fanatic and a strict teetotaller. On his training spins round the local fields at night Dai would be accompanied at first by his faithful dog, but being unable to keep the pace it ended up in its kennel, whilst Dai went round and round in the moonlight. Dai went on to play for Wales in Paris, when with Neath R.F.C. He returned to his native village, Hendy, astounded with the news that little children, 'so high', spoke French. All this in Welsh.

Dai later became a referee in West Wales, and a Llanelli international forward of the time recounts how Dai at half-time came up to him and said in Welsh, 'Give that Guy's Hospital forward a clout for me, he's constantly appealing "Oh Ref, offside".' The forward obliged, whereupon Dai walked up to the assailant and ceremoniously pointed to the pavilion changing room—to the ringing cheers of the 'impartial' Llanelli crowd. He was not sent off and what the crowd had not heard was Dai's remark, 'Kill the bastard next time.' The same Guy's player had expostulated that Dai's award of a try to the opposition was not valid: Dai's reply was 'Well buy the *Football Echo* tonight, and you'll find out in that.'

A contemporary player of Dai's time and a great character of the Llanelli team was Bobbie Evans. He claimed to be a gunman of some skill, bringing down 'jackadaws' by the score—this in the hearing of the local gun-toting, pheasant-shooting aristocracy in the lounge of the local hotel. Bobby lost an international cap when returning on the train from a Final Welsh Trial at Newport, in company with three of the 'Big Five' selection committee; he refused to carry the portmanteau of one of them and was not chosen for Wales.

Another character of Dai's era was Frank Evans, born and bred in the village of Dafen, just outside Llanelli town. As a player he was a bag of tricks on the wing, exploiting something which I have never seen since, and that was the dummy kick—ball held out in both hands in simulation of a kick and then accelerating past his turned opponent. He went north to Swinton and toured New Zealand, where in Christchurch he was accosted by a policeman, who had heard him speak in Welsh to a fellow player across the street. The policeman asked Frank where he came from. The reply was 'Dafen', an unknown village some 8,000 miles away. The policeman replied, 'Oh! I come from Felinfoel,' a village two miles from Dafen and associated with Phil Bennett and Barry John's parents.

There is a story about Barry John (the best fly-half I have seen in my time): on the morning of an England *v.* Wales game at Cardiff, a Welshman, pointing across the street, said to an Englishman 'Look, there's Barry John.' 'So what?' was the reply, 'He's not the Almighty.' 'No,' was the reply, 'but he's young yet.'

To return to Llanelli R.F.C. The twenties and thirties saw the legendary Albert Jenkins in his heyday—'the non pareil', the greatest three-quarter I've seen or played with. He was essentially a shy and reserved man, except in the dressing-room, where he showed a sense of humour both in Welsh and English. He was often 'browned-off' when accosted in the street by supporters—but there again rugby is a part of a pattern of life in South Wales—where dukes and dustmen play side by side.

Albert came into prominence first with the 38th Welsh Division in France in 1917-18. On being demobbed he soon made his mark, his first game for Llanelli being at Neath in September 1920. He was of compact build, five feet nine inches tall, deep chested, with powerful thighs and legs. He was always immaculately dressed on the football field with hair brushed back and polished boots. He was a startling contrast to the others, who played in a variety of shorts, often not washed from the previous Saturday.

His pace and dash for thirty yards was terrific, his punting, drop-kicking and place-kicking extraordinary, and withal his accurate passing was sharp and swiftly timed. He was a master at running diagonally at an opposing three-quarter line, compelling each player to pass until the unlucky recipient was hauled into touch. With facility, he could take the ball with one hand on the run and when bowled over he would regain his equilibrium with astounding agility.

Albert had a classical style which stamped all his movements, great in defence and brilliant in attack, in which he was a past master in making a dummy. I once saw his wing snatch at a pass, which wasn't there. Albert was also tough; I saw him knocked out only once, when at Stradey a young Cardiff full-back, who was to win immortal Rugby League fame, and Albert were both knocked out as Albert scored a try. Albert, in addition to his skill, was a steadying influence on his colleagues through his quiet and unobtrusive captaincy.

The Llanelli R.F.C. immediately after the Great War was on the crest of a wave, with many ardent and diverse supporters supporting the Scarlets at home and away in great numbers. The Llanelli crowd, fanatical, knowledgeable and witty, were the salt of the earth. Who else could advise a Barbarian player to go back to Barbaria? Many of them had nicknames, which were often essential with so many surnames like Jones, Thomas, Rees, Evans and Davies. Some nicknames were 'Tom Spots', 'Dai Salvation', 'Billy wants a wife', 'Tom Betsy' (after his wife), 'Will Up and Down', with one leg shorter than the other, 'Annie Aberdare' (the local prostitute), 'Jack Shrimps', and the local police-sergeant 'Twm Pen Taten' (Tom potato head). One local was known only as 'Billy Tidy', because his mother had been overheard to say what a tidy boy her son was—always took toilet-paper to work. Another was 'Dai O'Hesra', he having signed a printed letter to the local newspaper 'E. L. O'HESRA', which makes interesting reading backwards. Then there was 'Dai Substantial', the newly appointed English manager of the local steel-works, given the name because he told his foreman that he would not object to a nickname in order to prevent confusion 'as long as it was something substantial'. One of the best known of Llanelli supporters was 'Jimmy Daicco', who always turned up at Stradey Park wearing an appropriate symbol for a visiting team—a bunch of keys for Cross Keys, two dead crows dangling from the hip for black-jerseyed Neath, a white dead duck for Swansea and so on. Another ardent supporter was 'Idwal

Town Hall', who during the Second World War rushed into a council meeting shouting out the news: 'The Japs have taken Tokyo!' causing the meeting to be abandoned in consternation.

But the greatest character was 'Tosh' Evans, who on the field always entertained the crowd in the stand with an eccentric dance, and a juggling with a walking-stick and bowler hat, all interspersed with a two-fingered whistling. 'Tosh' was the cause of amazing scenes at St. Helens, Swansea, in October 1919, when Llanelli defeated Swansea there for the first time in twenty-three years by one try to nil. Llanelli town, cut off like the ancient Greek City-States, was the All-Welsh Cinderella compared with cosmopolitan Swansea and rivalry was intense. Llanelli supporters numbered 7,000 out of a 15,000 crowd. 'Tosh' affixed a scarlet-beribboned saucepan (the Llanelli emblem) to a crossbar. A Swansea supporter shook it off and carried it away in triumph and free-fights were the order of the day. One Llanelli supporter, who could be distinguished by his pink shirt, was 'Jamesie' Davies, who did some slamming, and five Swansea-ites fell like logs. The noble art learned by 'Jamesie' in the forces was serving him well. Thirty to forty fights were soon in progress but luckily the two teams took the field and order was restored.

2   *Early Schooldays*

I was one of eight children and had a happy childhood, even though we were not well off; indeed I remember having to wear my sister's button-up boots, but we were well fed, the staple meal being a broth of sheep's head and leeks, with vegetables. Bread, butter and cheese were quite common, but luxuries like oranges and prunes were non-existent.

We made our own fun, playing in the streets and fields, tip-cat (cat and dog), marbles, hop-scotch, rounders and strong-horses being great favourites. The last mentioned involved a line of six boys bent down shoulder to posterior against a wall and an opponent of the opposing team projecting himself by hand over the line of boys to land astride on an opponent's back. The team to land the farthest was the winner. Strangely enough, we never heard of slipped discs in those days. Cricket bats were home-made out of fencing purloined from local fields.

A fine treat was to be allowed to visit the local cinema, with ½d. worth of chips stuffed into the pocket, to watch silent-screen heroes and heroines. The weekly serial was a great feature in those days, each episode ending with 'To be continued' at a nail-biting climax. I still remember Pearl White as the heroine in 'The Exploits of Elaine'. It had an accompanying theme song thumped out on a piano: 'Elaine, Elaine, I love you all in vain, you are my moving-picture queen.'

Adolescents and grown-ups also made their own fun, playing quoits or fives against the pine-end of a house. Rat-catching was another diversion, the rats being caught in wire-cages and let loose to dogs, or penned in a barrel or empty railway truck to be despatched by the dogs.

Well-remembered schooldays began for me at the age of seven in 1913 at the local 'elementary school' down the road, where I was for five years. The headmaster, nicknamed 'Rusty' from his red beard, was a hard man. Perhaps he had to be in the climate of those days. He caned boys mercilessly and many a lad shivered as he entered the classroom. One late mark in the register resulted in four strokes of the cane across the hand; if you did not touch your cap to him on the road you received three or four strokes across the posterior, and one on the inside of the thigh. Truancy was no answer for he went out hunting for 'mitchers', as we called them, with a pack of boys.

Neither he nor his deputy, equally sadistic, was Welsh-speaking, as seventy per cent of his pupils were. The teaching of Welsh and in Welsh was, regrettably, forbidden by the 1870 Education Act, so our native tongue was not taught, nor our traditional Welsh folk-songs nor *The Land of my Fathers* (*Hen Wlad Fy Nhadau*).

'Rusty' did teach us gardening, as the school had two allotments, and this came in useful later on in life. Turnip-stealing from the allotments was an occasional peccadillo committed by myself and friend, the turnips being eaten raw as a delicacy. One evening we were nearly surprised by 'Rusty' and escaped only by diving through a hedge. The next day he innocently asked our class who were the socially-minded boys who had turned up to cultivate the plots, but we kept mum—the consequences would have been dire indeed—a caning, while we howled and grovelled in agony on the class-room floor.

I am a believer in corporal punishment to a limited extent; particularly for adolescent thugs and bully-boys, now only cautioned or put on probation for their crimes of violence: how they must laugh and how they repeat their acts of violation of the law. Social reformers have gone too far.

This is where the playing of rugby football is a catharsis of prime value—it has a great social and educational value, it moulds character and personality, and promotes and inculcates discipline, self-control, manners, deportment and co-operation. If more youths played rugby, we should have less violence and hooliganism, fewer hippies, Teds, Mods, Rockers, Hell's Angels and other selfish enemies of society.

I entered Llanelli County (Grammar) School, popularly known as the 'Intermediate', in September 1918. On my first day I was resplendent in a new suit bought by my mother the previous day in the 'Ready Made' shop, but I did not remain immaculate for long, being a grubby schoolboy with no scholastic ambitions, the playing of rugby football being my main concern.

The school consisted of about three hundred boys with a staff of varied personalities. I was lucky in having as a headmaster Griff Thomas, an ex-Jesus College Oxford graduate. I like the story of the visitor who entered the College Quadrangle and shouted out 'Is Dai Jones there?' and every window except two opened. Griff, a native of the town, was kind and understanding and never used the cane. He was a gentleman, 'a parfit gentle knight', who set us all a standard of behaviour, a pattern to copy.

Most of the staff were equally kind with inevitable schoolboy nicknames. The Second Master, called 'Tommy Dodge', was a wit who taught Maths to the fifth form. He acquired his pseudonym from his constant exhortation to boys not to dodge the firm tackling of a mathematical problem. He himself frequently dodged the issue, since when he illustrated the working out of an old G.C.E Maths problem on the blackboard, he copied it from a little pocket-book. If 'Tommy' deputised for an absent colleague, the lesson would be given over to telling of jokes by the boys, but as a safety-measure each joke had to be written down on a piece of paper and presented to 'Dodge', who read it out—if it were not naughty. In contrast the other maths master was a mental sadist in his extraction of an answer to a problem from a not-so-bright boy. Some boys literally fainted under the stress of his gruelling. His favourite method of dealing with a 'litter-bug' was to make the culprit tear a newspaper, or part of it, into very small pieces, throw them into the teeth of any air-current going, and make him pick them up one by one.

There was also 'Bumph', the history master, who was in charge of rugby football. He was a kind man, and no former pupil in the forces, who visited the School during the last war left without a gift of money. 'Tip' the Latin master was so nick-named for his frequent tips on how to memorise, mnemonics being a basic one. 'Doldrums', the Geography master was identified thus for his references in lessons to that geographical area on the globe. Another master was 'Siki', so called because of his swarthy resemblance to Battling Siki, world champion pugilist. 'Billy Boof', the woodwork master, was rather deaf but a proficient lip-reader who laid about him with a lath. 'Shiny' was so called from his glossy pomaded hair. 'Dai Rod' (Roderick), the chemistry master, was a dry wit but the daddy of them all was a late comer to the staff nicknamed 'Daddy', the most incompetent teacher I've known. He had been transferred to the School after a period as head-master of a Valley Grammar School because of his ineptitude and inability to maintain discipline. He had evolved a method of his own, which was to provide each of the two biggest boys in the classroom with a cudgel to belabour a noisy and talk-ative pupil at the adjuration, 'At him.' The last seen of him was in classroom one day, when he said 'I can't stand any more of this,' threw down his gown and left the class to its own devices.

A popular staff-member was the P.T. master, Capt. Jacobs, ex-gymnastics officer in the Army. With no gymnasium P.T. was taught on the school lawn in summer, we boys performing in our socks, self-conscious of holes and darns. In winter, the boys were turned out on the school rugby pitch with a rugby ball, the Captain meanwhile having retired to the nearby public house for a few pints of beer. When he returned, he achieved his ambition by becoming mine-host of the same pub.

There were virtually no school playing amenities. What a difference now; some schools are chromium-plated palaces with playing-fields and changing-quarters of the highest stan-dards on the ground—luxurious, in fact, with all mod-cons.

We changed in classrooms and trotted to our playing-field a short distance away in our boots. There were no white lines to demarcate the touch-line, only a groove carved out with a spade. On our return to school after the game, there were no hot and cold showers. Our only means of ablution in the school cloak-room was to slosh ourselves with cold water in water-basins. Soap, of raw carbolic type, was free, and many a sensitive face peeled afterwards.

Our only rugby pitch was on a pronounced slope. Many a ball was punctured behind the goal-posts on the spiked fencing. I was interested to see on a recent visit to Llanelli how the spikes are still flattened—the result of my efforts with a hammer! And I couldn't resist looking to see if my name was still carved out with a pen-knife on the red-brick portals of my old school—it was.

After gaining my School Certificate at Matriculation level in 1924, I was able to pursue a course of study for five years between 1924-9 at the University College of Wales at Singleton, Swansea. This was entirely due to the kindness of my brother Cliff, a steel-worker, who during the whole of this period maintained me. I now pay my tribute of everlasting gratitude to him. An outstanding feature of working-class life in those days in South Wales was the earnest desire of parents and families, heedless of sacrifice, to promote the education and career of an able child.

They were happy and carefree days at Swansea University College, when I looked at life through rose-coloured glasses. Numerically, it was a small college of approximately 350-400 students, of both sexes. On my last visit to the campus, comparatively recently, I got lost. Universities, nowadays, are too large in size and numerically. Like comprehensive schools they should be cut down drastically, if responsible and gregarious citizens are to be produced. In my day we were one large family.

Staff and students at the College were in accord, the polish of the former rubbing off on to the students. The Principal, Dr. Edwards, was a cultured man, often with psychological insight, turning a blind eye to the peccadilloes of the students. He was ably supported by the polished and urbane Professor Thomas ('Prof. Thom') the head of the English department and Dean of the Faculty of Arts. I think they were rather amused with the rugger students' activities and escapades: indeed, in after years 'Prof Thom' drily remarked to me that 'the students now are only schoolboys and schoolgirls.'

Of rugger escapades there were many, especially during inter-coll week, when the colleges of Aberystwyth, Cardiff, Swansea and Bangor played one another. At Bangor we stayed at the 'Railway Hotel', when we ran wild in our callow high spirits. I was amused to observe in the foyer of the hotel on the Sunday morning, after our previous day's game, a gentleman in morning dress plus bowler-hat plus brief-case but without shoes—they had been spirited away in the night, when covered with blankets we had acted the part of Red Indians with accompanying war-cries.

One person not amused was the hotel porter, son of the local mayor, for on the Monday morning on our return to College the rugger XV were summoned to the Senate Room to be interviewed by the Principal and the Dean of the Faculty of Arts. The Principal gravely informed us there had been complaints about our behaviour, particularly those in Room 8, who had told the porter to 'Buzz off you son of a bachelor' or words to that effect. The Principal handed me the letter of complaint and asked me who had been the occupants of Room 8. Sheepishly I had to confess that it had been myself and friend, whereupon the Principal with a twinkle in his eye said, 'Gentlemen, please do not do it again; you may all go.' He and the Dean departed to the strains of 'Oh! why were they born so beautiful? Oh! why were they born at all?' Yes, we were a high-spirited lot, but not destructive.

Our most glamorous and important fixture was against Bristol University away. On one occasion there our scrum-half and captain was Harry Beynon who, when harried by an opposing wing-forward protested 'When did they let you out of the Zoo?' I was having a particularly good, clean, robust game, and at half-time Harry was called over by the referee with the request that he 'tell' that black-haired forward (meaning myself). Harry asked the referee, 'Yes but tell him what?' to receive the reply 'I don't know but tell him.'

My career at Swansea University was not all beer and skittles: I worked hard at my studies, often working into the small hours of the morning to catch up on time lost through playing rugby. When I was sitting for my degree, I and some other students engaged in 'all-nighters', sporadically studying all night, but it's not a course I would recommend to students: the answer is steady work throughout the year, though I couldn't bring myself to swot much during the vacations.

Owing to shyness girls did not interest me much and I escaped from their charms. But this was not the fate of a newly arrived student—a 'fresher' seduced by the wife of one of our professors, he being much too old and humourless for her. About thirty years of age, she was of French extraction, vivacious, dark and beautiful and undoubtedly over-sexed. She pursued students at college dances and like functions avidly and lured a few of them to bed. How I escaped I don't know, but the young fresher was not so lucky. An anonymous phone call gave her husband the tip-off, and returning home he caught the student and his wife in bed. Divorce proceedings followed and the student was expelled ignominiously. He followed her to Paris, only to be sent packing by her mother. Later, he wrote a sad and pathetic letter to the periodical *John Bull* denouncing her as 'The Siren of the East'.

My last year at College was spent on a teacher's training certificate course, which, apart from teaching practice, was a farce, lectures being all theory and far removed from the actualities of teaching. My teaching practice was done at a Secondary Modern school at Llanelli, which I attended on two days a week. The headmaster and staff were kind and helpful, and I learned a lot about the hard graft of teaching and how to deal with boys in the classroom.

The acme of success was achieved in the last week of my training course, when I had to engage in teaching lessons before a Board of Education Inspector with a view to my being granted a Teacher's Certificate. I think I passed through native wit and improvisation. All boys know a rookie and try to take it out of him. One of the questions asked me by a boy was, 'Please Sir, what is a eunuch?' With great mental agility I answered 'A member, or shall I say dismembered member, of a Sheik's harem, the guardian of his indoor games.' I gained my certificate, though an apocryphal story went round the college that I had been giving a crit-lesson on the Spanish Armada, and after a while, having been pestered by a little boy continually on how big a ship was a galleon, replied in exasperation with arms thrown wide, 'a big ship, a bloody big ship.' And so it was said I gained my Teacher's Certificate by virtue of 'graphic and vivid and illuminating illustration'.

During College days I also played for Llanelli Rugby Club and two games stand out in my memory. The first was against Newport at Llanelli in December 1926. There had been an element of bitterness and bad blood between the two clubs since 1910, when the Llanelli Rugby Club sued a Newport newspaper for what they alleged was a scandalous and libellous report of the game between the two clubs, Llanelli being accused of dirty and foul play. At the end of the legal action, the Llanelli Club were awarded one farthing damages and ordered to pay for the costs of the case, which were over £5,000. At the same time as all this unpleasantness Newport R.F.C. cancelled fixtures with Llanelli.

Let us go on to the resumed fixture then. It was expected that a big crowd would attend, but on the morning of the game it was discovered that a portion of the pitch in front of the stand was frost-bound. The Llanelli Committee showed great ingenuity and resource: loads of hot hops from the local brewery were despatched to the Stradey ground and scattered over the affected area. Jack Frost vanished and the game was played. The game itself was a ding-dong struggle ending in a draw, having been played in the best of spirits. In this respect, a verse by George Boots, the old Newport and Welsh forward, is worth quoting. It's an admirable summing up of rugby football:

> Life's happiness—the rarest joy
> Is not in wealth or fame,
> But in the friendships that we make
> And the way we play the game.

The second game that stands out in my mind at this time in 1926 was when Llanelli Club defeated the touring Maoris at Stradey Park by 3-0, the only Welsh side to do so, though Pontypool later defeated the tourists in an unofficial fixture. What a remarkable record Llanelli has against touring sides: it's the Welsh '*hwyl*' (emotional verve) and electric atmosphere at Stradey; it is concomitant with all that is Welsh—ten of the Llanelli XV that played the Maoris were Welsh speaking. Yes, the atmosphere at Stradey Park is certainly Cymric and unique. Even back in 1923 a Leicester sports correspondent moaned about the behaviour of the Llanelli crowd, saying 'There must have been one thousand self-constituted referees on the ground, enough to bewilder the strongest of referees and visiting players.'

I remember the Maori game well, Sid Hay, the Llanelli wing, scoring the try. I recollect having to leave the field for fifteen minutes to have my cut head treated by St. John Ambulance men, and returning to play with head swathed in bandages like an Indian. The Maoris were not too gentle in rucking in loose mauls and my thighs from groin to knee were scored with dirt-embedded stud gashes. Here, I pass on a tip much used in those days by tin-plate workers gashed on the hands at their rolls—I used an ointment of resin and palm-oil mixed, called 'Cwyr Crydd' (cobblers wax) locally; it's not a remedy I would advocate nowadays, though. Use one of the proprietary brand of antiseptics, which can be bought at any chemist.

I made amends to some extent by returning to play for Llanelli in 1934, playing for the club on school vacations for four seasons. A game which stands out in my memory is the one in which I played for Llanelli at the end of season 1934 at Aberavon. The latter had a two years' ground record to defend and were a hard nut to crack. The game was a typical Welsh local derby, the like of which is not seen in England, except perhaps in the West Country. I had a particularly good game in a match which, to put it mildly, was rather robust. We won by a try and a dropped goal kicked by Dai

Right, the 21-year-old Watcyn Thomas wearing his first Welsh International Cap in 1927

Below, the Llanelli XV who defeated the Maoris in 1926. Captain is Ifor Jones

Wales *v.* Scotland at Cardiff in 1927. *Back row, left to right*, Morgan Moses (Touch-judge), E. Jenkins, I. Jones, T. Arthur, H. T. Phillips, Watcyn Thomas, J. H. John, T. W. Lewis, W. H. Jackson (Referee); *middle row*, J. Roberts, R. Harding, B. O. Male (Capt.), B. R. Turn-bull, W. A. Williams; *front*, G. Richards, J. D. Bartlett and W. J. Delahay

John—a far superior fly-half to the highly regarded Bennie Osler of South Africa in my opinion.

Passions run high in such a game among the spectators and two incidents stand out in my mind. The first was when I observed an incensed Aberavon supporter wielding a hatchet and trying to climb over the fencing to get at me. The second incident occurred when the final whistle went and an under-sized Aberavon supporter rushed up to me and looked up and said, 'Call yourself a —— schoolmaster,' and scampered away like a frightened rabbit.

I must say that at the conclusion of the game the Aberavon crowd in the stand gave us a standing ovation, though I doubt if the Aberavon international forward Ned Jenkins joined in. He sported a black eye on police-duty after the game, the injury being inflicted when I accidentally poked my elbow into his eye in the line-out.

We played by natural ability in those days, not as cultured theorists, but I must say that the coaching of players nowadays by such as Carwyn James can only be good for the game and has raised its standard tremendously. But we must beware of natural flair and innate genius and improvisation being subdued and canalised into sterility.

I played my first game for Swansea R.F.C. against Cardiff at home early in 1928 and represented the Club on vacations from teaching at St. Helens, Lancs, until the end of 1933. It was not my first game on the ground, for I had played for Llanelli Schoolboys against the Swansea Town team as wing-three-quarter in January 1920. Incidentally, later on in my teaching career, as rugger coach, I was a great believer in the first and second XV players, in practices, playing some time or other in all positions, even as prop-forward, to give them a knowledge, feeling and understanding of the game.

The Swansea atmosphere on the field of play and in the crowd was as different from that of Llanelli's as chalk from cheese. Swansea City, like Cardiff, is a cosmopolitan city and not truly representative of the Welsh way of life, though it is Welsh in sentiment. To hear Welsh spoken freely you have to go into the hinterland, into the valleys.

It is more Welsh than Cardiff, though, which reminds me that only last year I was engaged in conversation with a Cardiffian in the lounge-bar of an hotel in Whitchurch, the Cardiff suburb, on the morning of the Wales *v.* England game, my friends and I having stayed the night. On hearing after his enquiring that we were from Llanelli, his comment was, 'Oh! you're Taffies,' which made me think that he regarded us as troglodytes having just arrived from the valleys—somewhat akin to the cave-dwellers of ancient times.

The Swansea Club was a fine one with a great tradition. In its time it had been well-nigh invincible in many seasons and had produced some fine players. In 1893-4 the great W. J. Bancroft, as full-back, was captain, and he played for Wales on thirty-three occasions—no mean feat, as there were no tours abroad then. He played for Wales against England at Dewsbury (no Rugby League then) in February 1890, the team being the first Welsh side to defeat England. A small, agile man, he could easily avoid the ponderous forwards of those days. He was a fine punter of the ball and it is interesting to note that in practice he would place the ball at an uprooted corner flag and by using side and wind kick it over the cross-bar.

Another Swansea old-stager with whom I became friendly was Frank 'Genny' Gordon, captain of Swansea in 1904-5, when the 'All-Whites' for the first time in their history were undefeated, winning twenty-eight games and playing a draw in four. Another great club player in those days was W. J. Trew, who could play anywhere behind the scrum. He played for Wales on twenty-nine occasions between 1900-13. I don't know if Swansea 'invented' the wing-forward, but it was a pointer of things to come when in season 1908-9 Ivor Morgan, a Welsh international back row forward, scored eighteen tries for the club.

Now back to my playing days with Swansea. We were a happy crew under a genial secretary in Bert Palmer, an ex-player. We had an affable chairman of the selection committee, generally known by his nickname 'Dai Piss'. Trevor Davies, who had played for Swansea and Maesteg R.F.C., was also a selector. He used to sum up the belligerent but not so brave player as 'The hold me back, let me go' type.

A prominent player was Rowe Harding (eventually Judge Rowe Harding), in his time captain of Swansea, Cambridge University and Wales and a British Lion in South Africa. Jack Elwyn Watkins of Abercrave was an ex-captain, who when he played occasionally in the centre had as his wing D. P. Manley, whose reaction to a critical crowd was to give them the 'V' sign. Others included J. H. John, capped eight times for Wales, and D. R. Jenkins (Resolven) whose uncle was the legendary Dai St. John, who won an immortal place in Welsh legend for his fighting qualities in the Boer War, his favourite method of despatching his enemies being to bayonet them and throw them over his shoulder. Dai Parker was a great wit who played for the British Lions in New Zealand in 1930. Will Clement, prop-forward, nicknamed 'Gallant' for his frequent refusal to go off the field when injured. Other players were W. J. Trew Junior (son of the immortal W. J.) and Jack Rees, Captain in 1931-2. He was a great humorist and an asset in promoting team spirit. Will Davies, wing-forward from the Amman Valley and nicknamed 'Skeely', who scored the try for Wales against South Africa in 1931 (the first try scored by Wales against the Springboks) and genial Claude Davey were other players, both devastating tacklers.

Claude Davey was the crash-tackler in excelsis. When he tackled he took off and flew through the air. Wales won a historic victory against New Zealand at Cardiff Arms Park in 1936 and one of the prime architects, or perhaps destroyer would be a better description, was Claude Davey for his bone-crushing tackles of one of the New Zealand five-eight's, their danger man. I met Claude after the game, and conversing in Welsh he expressed a dim view of his All-Black opponent, the reason being the reaction of the New Zealander. I pursued the matter and Claude explained that after the first and second tackle his opponent had called out 'You bastard.' I asked

Claude what his opponent said after the third tackle and Claude's succinct reply was 'Nothing.'

Another prominent Swansea player of this time was Joe White of Morriston, not over endowed with intelligence, dull as a sledge as we say in South Wales, but game as a pebble on the field. After one of Swansea's home games Joe went on the beer and missed his last bus home to Morriston four miles away. Joe was kindly accommodated by the landlord of the Bush Hotel for nowt for the night, but the landlord, Dai Thomas, was somewhat rueful the next morning for Joe had got up in the middle of the night to go to the bathroom and on seeing his reflection in the wardrobe mirror had lashed out and smashed the mirror. Joe had been under the misapprehension that he was looking at a forward of the Llanelli team against whom he had played earlier on.

On another occasion Joe had missed the last bus home and decided to walk home to Morriston. Within a hundred yards or so from home, Joe found that he had no matches and asked an oncoming pedestrian for a light: in the process of igniting he turned round to shield himself from the wind, and having lit his cigarette walked back all the way to Swansea, some four miles.

Another Swansea forward with whom I played was the intelligent front row man Tom Day, intelligent because he had a flair for opening up play for his backs. He and I were boozing pals and for that came under the displeasure of the Welsh Union and its secretary, the martinet Walter Rees, J.P. We were always late after trial matches in claiming our travelling expenses, having been delayed in the bar, no fault of ours, of course. Tommy was fond of relating how he went on two occasions to claim his travelling expenses at Swansea. Tommy lived four miles away at Skewen and Walter Rees eight miles or so at Neath. The Oxford and Cambridge trialists were putting in claims on the first occasion for between six and eight pounds, so Tommy rather daringly up-graded his expenses to 7/6. The reply he got from Walter was 'Good God man! Where do you come from—Moscow?'

The highlight of my Swansea playing days was the occasion when the club went on tour at the end of the 1928-9 season to the south of France to play Auch and Tarbes in the Haute-Pyrenees. We were a young and high-spirited band of players. Few had been abroad before and few could speak French, so it was astonishing when we received replies to queries in English. One of our players in a spirit of devilment accosted a Parisienne in the street in Paris and asked, 'Excuse me, do you fornicate?' to receive the reply, 'Yes, like a queen.'

We stayed but one night in Paris, on our way south, and a practical joke was played on one of our young players, who had visited a brothel. On his return to our hotel he was persuaded that he had picked up venereal disease, and to prove it he was asked to urinate into a chamber-pot. Unbeknown to him it contained a sprinkling of permanganate of potash, and when his urine turned red he was so distraught that he went pale and almost fainted.

The highlight of our tour, however, was our visit to the south of France, when we played Auch and Tarbes. We won both games. At Auch, fourteen miles west of Toulouse, we were entertained regally, being wined and dined, as only the French know how. Each player before the kick-off was introduced to the crowd. I regret to say that acting on our information some fictitious claims were made, almost every player being an international, or if not, would be 'next year'. But we were not barbarians, and in the morning visited one of the finest Gothic cathedrals in France, it being perched on a hill, and accessible only by a flight of two hundred steps. Despite this 'training' we won our game in the afternoon.

We went on to play Tarbes, an ancient town a hundred miles south-west of Toulouse and famous for its twelfth-century domed cathedral, which we visited. Tarbes has historical associations, for here in 1814 Wellington gained a victory over the French under Marshal Soult. It was the birthplace of Marshal Ferdinand Foch (1851-1929), who became supreme general of both the French and British troops in March 1918, and who stemmed the final German attack and brought the Great War to a successful end.

We also paid a flying visit to Lourdes, the birthplace of St. Bernadette, to whom the Roman Catholic world believes the Virgin Mary revealed herself when Bernadette was fourteen years of age. Though not a great believer in religion, I found the experience moving, especially the sight of so many infirm pilgrims with arms outstretched affirming faith and beseeching a cure.

We returned home after sights and experiences we would never have gained but for the playing of rugby football—another example of its educational value.

4 *At St. Helens*

I taught and lived in St. Helens, Lancashire, from January 1929 until July 1937 and spent there some of the happiest days of my life. St. Helens was a town of comparatively modern growth with an enormous glass industry (Pilkington's), copper-smelting works, foundries and chemical manufacturing works. Coal was mined in the outskirts.

The town was only half an hour's journey from Liverpool, and what a contrast! Liverpool was a cosmopolitan centre, quite sophisticated, whose inhabitants spoke in a high nasal tone but St. Helens was real Lancashire with its own patois and provincial dialect. Although it had a population of over 100,000, people were familiar and always gave a friendly salutation in the streets. I still regard it as my second home.

My first impression of the town was not a favourable one. It was a product of the Industrial Revolution, anything but beautiful and my heart sank a little as I walked up from the railway station to the Town Hall, for an interview with the Chief Education Officer and Headmaster of the local grammar school. At the Town Hall Square I did observe a statuette of St. Helen in its wall niche. Incidentally St. Helens had a large Roman Catholic population, of Irish descent but never did I encounter any religious bigotry in the town. A few of the inhabitants were descendants of old English Catholics of pre-Reformation days but the town was mainly Protestant, Church of England with some non-conformists.

Back to the interview, the outcome being that with another South Walian I had to give a practical demonstration of my teaching ability and suitability by taking a class, the next day, of young lads, with the headmaster sitting in attendance.

Readers might think that I degraded myself by undergoing such a test, but it must be remembered that teaching posts were difficult to get in those days, three hundred applicants not being uncommon. I had applied for a post in my home town, Llanelli, but to obtain a post contenders had to canvass the County Council Education Committee members by travelling around in a taxi or motor-car to curry support; I could not bring myself to do such a thing.

The result of the practical teaching test was that I was offered the post, on condition that I toned down my Welsh accent, which I promised to do, but I'm proud to say that today after forty-six years' residence in England, I'm still asked 'What part of Wales do you come from?'

The unsuccessful Welsh applicant and I celebrated my appointment by touring Liverpool hotels and pubs that night before returning to the Fleece Hotel, St. Helens, for bed and breakfast. I had cause to remember my Welsh applicant in subsequent years, for K., as I shall designate him, proved to be a 'con-man' of the highest order, twice persuading me on international days at Cardiff to part with a pound note with the specious excuse he would soon be back. I never saw him again but, somehow, I did not learn, for on another occasion I was accosted by a townsman in the same hotel and parted with a pound on his quoting the names of my brothers and sisters and with the promise he would call in at my home the next night, and with the request that I should not tell my family of his borrowing—he would be so ashamed! There's one born every minute but you learn by experience.

My headmaster was big-eared, balding, and a sadist, carrying a cane under his gown with which he belaboured boys who failed to answer a question. It's indeed surprising that he was not sued by any parents for his cruelty. He took great pleasure in inflicting pain physical and mental and the staff did not go unscathed. His favourite trick was to walk around the quadrangle, listen outside the classroom door, enter and sit down when you were teaching, and subject you afterwards to a series of criticisms of your teaching. The staff evolved a system, whereby they were warned that the headmaster was on the prowl. If you were late arriving at school in the morning you had to report to him, and on the ringing of a bell you entered his room and stood before him, he sitting at his desk, and explained why you were late—just like an erring schoolboy.

But we were a happy lot despite the Head and a silly personal feud between the heads of English and Latin. The second master and chairman of the staff common room was Tom Carr, nicknamed 'spatty' by the boys because he always wore spats. He taught history and his method of teaching was to make the boys transcribe notes he had written on the board—frowned upon now but he got results. The English master was somewhat fond of holding boys by the hand and he, too, got matriculation results by circulating among his fifth-formers printed notes on set books—he called them 'bibles' but it was hardly teaching. The French master was a jovial Scot, who naturally had the nickname of 'Jock'—he liked his drops of whisky but did not go around the school grounds at recess, sipping it behind bushes as a master I once knew did. The physics master named Webb, not unnaturally was nicknamed 'spider', and the maths master, Powell, 'woof-woof' because of his manner of speaking. He insisted on his name being pronounced 'Pole'. The chemistry master, a most sensible and delightful man, was called 'chemy-Les' after his Christian name. The P.T. master was nicknamed 'Hell-Fire', since he believed the playing of card games, even bridge, was the invention of the devil and the way to hell. The Geography master was called 'Dick', he had a red nose and today would be called 'Rudolph' I suppose after Rudolph, the red-nosed reindeer. Incidentally he was a teetotaller. The Janitor was called 'Timber-toes', he having lost some in the Great War, and I, of course was called 'Taffy'. Last but not least was Kermode, the music master, a Great War veteran who had been promoted to commissioned rank on the battlefield, so high were the casualties. He produced many a Gilbert and Sullivan light opera, feminine characters being portrayed by boys, of course, for the mixing of the sexes was frowned upon in those days. Drinking in the town was also frowned upon by the headmaster, but I managed to escape his veto when he told me in his study that only 'certain' hotels could be patronised—I did not ask him which and carried on. Policemen were under the same restraint in town, which reminds me of the policeman on duty who slipped unobtrusively into the mews at the back of a 'local' where the landlord had deposited a pint of beer on a shelf for the policeman's consumption. It was dark and the copper came out smacking his lips with the remark 'Some good hops in that beer'—but the hops were black-beetles.

The town was full of characters, who told many a diverting story. I liked the one about the two old ladies who met in the main street outside the church, the bells of which were clanging away. One of the ladies was slightly deaf, and on being told by her friend, 'Aren't the bells beautiful?' replied, 'Will you please speak up, I can't hear you for them bloody bells.'

John Turner was a character, who used to ask people to look at his new watch, and when they did so, looking at its works, a pea would strike them in the face. It was done by his squirting the pea between his teeth, and he only desisted from his playfulness, when told that the pea could strike the curious one in the eye. Chuck H—— was a corporation official, who after having been bitten by dogs, when he was collecting rents, invented an electrified walking-stick, which he poked at the dogs: he suffered no more attacks.

Two of my stories are associated with public houses. There was one amazing landlord, who when proffered a shilling, florin or half-crown or even a 5/- piece, on his return with the order, would produce the correct change out of his other hand. No one knew how he did it—he must have been psychic. The other story concerned with drinking ale is the one relating to a headmaster in the old days before buses ran to outlying villages. His school was situated on top of a hill not far from St. Helens and overlooking the railway station below, which could be viewed from the smoke-room window of the local inn. The wily headmaster, knowing the times of arrival of all trains, would scrutinise each descending passenger, and on being assured that it was not a stranger who could possibly be one of H.M. Inspectors, carried on with his drinking, which was in school time. Between this village and Aintree outside Liverpool, there were more hares to the square mile than any other area in England, but woe-betide poachers caught red-handed.

To the north of the town on the way to Wigan, by way of contrast, were cesspools and brooks into which the noxious wastes of the local factories were drained. A favourite method among locals for 'curing' whooping-cough was to take their progeny to this derelict area and make them poke around the pools with walking-sticks—the old 'uns believed and swore that the arising vapour effected a cure.

In 1929 I played for St. Helens Old Boys (now just St. Helens) and believe I'm the only rugby international the club can claim. They were a grand lot of lads with a hardworking and faithful committee—all amateurs. Great was the furore when one of them turned professional by joining St. Helens Recreation, one of the two local Rugby League clubs. So horrified was my headmaster that he harangued the whole school on the iniquity of the move. The annual dinner of the Old Boys was held in a local hotel, the menu consisting only of Lancashire hot-pot—you should try it as made by a Lancastrian. Another delicacy I enjoyed was a sandwich of finely chopped Spanish onion and grated cheese. Better than the so-called ploughman's lunch of today. Unbeknown to the Welsh Rugby Union I trained on the St. Helens Recs. ground, mixing freely with the players. Three great forwards of theirs were Smith, Fildes and Mulvanney, called the Three Musketeers and the terror of the opposition. Mulvanney was a great character and as strong as any man I've known—woe betide a policeman who intruded into the dressing-room for he would be hoisted on to a big hook behind the door and left there to dangle helplessly. On his retirement Mulvanney became landlord of a local public house, and if you were pestered by a scrounger he had a novel way of getting rid of him: he would tinkle a bicycle bell in his private apartments and say you were required on the phone, whereupon, having answered it you made your escape.

Welshmen were prominent players in the town rugby league. One of them was almost bald, no chicken by any means. He had bluffed the club into signing him on by producing the birth-certificate of a much younger friend of his, of the same name, who lived in the same valley. Some Welsh players have had secret trials with Rugby League clubs unbeknown to the Welsh Union. One of them, who was not a success, claimed £20 in expenses and when his claim was queried and examined, it included train fare and taxi to the ground; when the club secretary expostulated that a bus would have carried him to the ground, the secret trialist exclaimed, 'If you had the rheumatics like me, you would have taken a taxi too!'

While in St. Helens I saw many a League game, mainly in mid-week, and on some Saturdays, when I was unfit to play Rugby Union with Waterloo R.F.C. Rugby League was not a game to which I could take a liking, for it had too much of a sameness and predictability, with none of the fluidity of Rugby Union. I speak of those days when resident in St. Helens. The Rugby League have tried to introduce more variety into the game but basically it's still the same. Then, after each tackle, a player was allowed to get up, tap the ball along the ground with his foot if only an inch or two in a forward direction, and restart the game; his colleagues meanwhile being lined up in support behind him and his opponents lying well up in defence. So the game was renewed from scratch (as it is now) and there was no variety stemming from line-out and quick heeling from loose mauls, when opponents can be overlapped. Scrums were a farce, with the three front row forwards standing almost upright when the ball was thrown in, with the middle man (hooker or 'striker' as they called it) ending up prostrate on the ground. Possession was essential, for successful results counted for bonus money, and I must admit that the resultant deft handling of the ball by backs and forwards combined was the acme of rhythm. Knocks-on meant loss of possession and this skill is something which Rugby Union forwards should cultivate.

Some South Wales rugby players still 'go north', but in lesser numbers, since unemployment there is not so rife as in the bad old days and Rugby Union playing is a strand in the pattern of life in South Wales; going Rugby League would mean giving up much that you love. Regrettably, there is still an undefinable hiatus between ex-Rugby League players who return home and the natives, but this state of affairs is changing and I've even seen ex and current League players in Union clubhouses in the Midlands.

5 _International Rugby_

It is the ambition of every rugby-minded Welsh boy to play for Wales and I was no exception, so I went on my way to achieve it. Many of my friends in England, where I have resided for forty-six years, have bemoaned the fact that the flame of patriotism does not burn so fiercely in the hearts of Englishmen. For me, Welsh was the language of the hearth: Wales my Fatherland, Land of My Fathers, _Henwlad fy Nhadau._ And what greater ambition, then, than to play against and defeat England?

I went on to play for Wales on fourteen occasions, and so some games must stand out in my memory. The first international in which I played was against England at Twickenham in 1927 at the age of twenty. It was definitely a hoodoo ground for Wales, being opened in 1910, when A. D. Stoop was the England captain. Between the years 1900-9, regarded as the golden era of Welsh rugby, Wales won the Triple Crown on six occasions. But the rot set in in 1910, when England won by 13-6, and again won in 1912 and 1914. After the Great War the Twickenham Bogey gathered momentum and Welsh defeats continued. England enjoying a period of emphatic dominance between 1923-31, when they won seven games and drew two.

Fate and the elements invariably seemed to favour England; in 1923 Wales were caught napping in the first minute of play as England kicked off against a gale; forward H. L. Price, following up, tried to drop a goal—the ball was blown back into his hands, and he had but to walk over the line to score a try. England added a dropped goal to the try and won 7-3, so the stage was set for my début there in 1927, leading up to the demolition of the Twickenham Bogey in 1933.

During the locust years Welshmen prayed fervently that Wales would win at Twickenham. Prayers were offered up to Heaven by members of all religious denominations each year that this be the day of retribution. Dr. Johnson, the sage of Lichfield, once said that 'Patriotism is the last refuge of a scoundrel', in which case all Welshmen were scoundrels of the deepest dye.

The preparation for the great day went on for a full year ahead. Collections to cover travelling expenses were made weekly in pubs, clubs and chapel vestries from young and old alike—it was not so much a case of 'See Naples and die' as 'Be there on the day'.

The great trek to Twickenham began on the Friday prior to the game, with the old G.W.R. running excursions from all parts of Wales up to 5.30 a.m. On the day, refreshments, solid and liquid were laid on, not all supporters being sober on the morning of the match or after. Indeed, for one supporter, bibulous refreshment had been too much and a doctor had to be called in because he asserted most emphatically that snakes and pink elephants were crawling up the wall.

It is as well to point out that Twickenham has vagaries that often lead to the defeat of visiting international XVs. Bounded on three sides by stands, it is a ground of atmospheric eddies and whirlpools, which make passing and kicking go fortuitously astray. But above all, it is the electric atmosphere that unnerves the man playing in his first international there. Raucous shouts, jeers and cheers rebound from the roofs of the stands, so that there is a constant roar in the ears of the players down below—enough to daunt and unsettle the most experienced of club players.

Tension builds up in the dressing-room before the game, visits to the toilet being frequent. It is a ground when familiarity with its vagaries counts and it's not surprising that a great number of players have played in only one international there, even though they have had wide experience in club, county and trial games. The initiate is inclined to charge around like a tormented bull, instead of canalising his energies. I speak of forwards mainly, and that is the way, I think, how I played there in my first international, the conservation of energy and application of skill at the right place and right time coming later. I hasten to add that backs out in the glare of exposure must suffer accordingly.

To the game of 1927 itself: I can only say through the mists of time that the Twickenham Bogey persisted, despite the fact that Wales had a nucleus of the fine 1926 side. I must pay tribute here to the way our captain, Ossie Male of Cardiff, looked after his players before and after the game, an example I strove to emulate later, when I captained the Welsh XV—a captain should be guide, philosopher and friend.

As I have said the Bogey persisted, for Dai Jones (Newport), one of our front-row forwards had to retire from the conflict after only twenty minutes' play with a broken collar-bone, and W. C. Powell, our scrum-half, was crocked before half-time, though he continued to play on. Wales were defeated by 11-9 but England's score included one penalty goal, one goal from a mark and one try only, one of England's goals bouncing off the cross-bar, after hesitating whether to fall over on the scoring side or not. In contrast to the one try scored by England, Wales scored two. The object of the game is to score tries, so the Bogey was well and truly alive.

Two years elapsed and I played my second international at Twickenham in January 1929. Wales, who had failed to lower the English colours on seven previous occasions were a young side of little experience. England included R. W. Smeddle and Carl Aarvold, both of Cambridge University, on the right flank, Colin Laird (Harlequins) at fly-half and in the forwards R. Cove-Smith (K.C.H.), captain, Roy Foulds and H. G. Periton (both of Waterloo), grand old Sam Tucker, a stevedore from Bristol as hooker, and ominously for us, H. Wilkinson (Halifax), as open side wing-forward. Carl Aarvold subsequently became a famous judge, ending up as Recorder of

London. We were to meet again in 1933, when Wales won at headquarters.

The Welsh captain, as wing-forward, was Ivor Jones (Llanelli) and our hooker A. F. Bowdler of Cross-Keys, whose dedication was such that I remember his playing for Wales at Cardiff one Saturday and returning immediately after the game to work underground in the coal-mine. In the pack we also had R. Jones (London Welsh) of Welsh-Japanese parentage, whose brother had played for Wales two years previously, when he played for Northampton. At full-back was the unknown Jack Bassett, to be known subsequently as 'The Rock of Gibraltar', and in front of him three inexperienced varsity players in the backs. What a fetish the Welsh selectors had for Oxford and Cambridge in those days.

Before the game, Welsh rugby enthusiasm was seen at its maximum—in town and on the ground. In the Strand and Piccadilly could be seen hundreds of Welshmen, wearing their national emblems and full of hope and confidence. At the ground, the stands on either side were given a blaze of colour by the red rosettes and berets worn by the Welsh followers. There was an amusing incident when one of the Welsh supporters attempted to fix a leek on one of the uprights. A policeman who ran towards him was loudly booed by the crowd, but boos were changed to cheers when it was seen that the policeman had gone to give him a leg-up.

As to the game itself, I regret to say that Wales lost by 8-3. There were 60,000 present when the teams fielded for inspection by the Prince of Wales. The genius of Aarvold and the superiority of the English in the scrums gave England a first-half lead of 3-0, the try being scored by Wilkinson. In this half England in the tight obtained the ball four times out of five, something I was to remedy later in my international career by quick heeling from loose mauls. The cause of Wales was not enhanced by the play of their half-backs in this half. Several of Wick Powell's passes from the scrum were unusually wild; he was a wayward genius but he hadn't much chance and the play of his fly-half, of Oxford University, included in the Welsh XV after a great final trial performance was disappointing. Were trials any good? I don't think so; the present squad system allied to club performances is the answer.

In the second half, the Welsh forwards were going great guns after fifteen minutes but England then increased their lead. Laird, receiving from a scrum forty yards out, broke through brilliantly and Wilkinson was up again to take his pass and score a try, which was converted by Wilson. Within a minute, however, came a score for Wales, and a more magnificent effort had never before been seen on the ground in an international. The young Welsh right wing Jack Morley (Newport) received the ball forty yards out, cut in towards the centre of the field and then, showing great pace, cut out again to the right, and with the English defence beaten crossed wide out: a self-made score. Morley subsequently became famous in the Rugby League code as well. Another distinct success was Jack Bassett, the Welsh full-back.

It was a magnificent game, in which everyone lasted the full eighty minutes, and England deserved their victory, being the greater opportunists. So the Twickenham spell still held.

The Bogey persisted in 1931 but Wales came nearer to destroying it than they had since the ground was opened in 1910. Both sides were composed of experienced players, with Wales having 'The Rock' Jack Bassett at full-back and captain of the side with T. E. Jones-Davies and crash-tackler Claude Davey in the centre, and those great wings Ronnie Boon and Jack Morley on the flanks. At scrum-half we had Wick Powell and up in the front row first-cap Tom Day and timeless Archie Skym. The back row was composed of myself as number eight, Norman Fender (Cardiff), a skilled co-operator with his backs, and Arthur Lemon (Neath) as blind side forward. Many stories can be told about Lemon—a famous Irish forward once vowed he would turn him into an orange, but it was the Irishman who was carried off with a painful rump injury.

England had Carl Aarvold in the centre with McCanlis of Gloucester as his co-centre and the brilliant Jim Barrington

(Bristol) as fly-half. In the forwards England had as hooker grand old Sam Tucker (Bristol) a stevedore by trade, and one of the few artisans who played for England in those days. In the back row, in contrast to Sam, England had P. D. Howard of Oxford and Old Millhilians, who later became a great advocate of moral rearmament and a crusader on its behalf. Most unfortunately for Wales, England in the forwards included B. H. Black (Blackheath), an ace goal kicker.

As usual, the game at headquarters was not without drama. In the preliminaries before the kick-off there was the usual affixing of a leek on one of the cross-bars by a Welsh supporter, who coolly conversed with the police-officer below who had tried to prevent his escalation. To the cheers of the huge Welsh band of supporters, their compatriot after descending was able to escape the clutches of converging bobbies by a series of side-steps, worthy of a Welsh three-quarter, to disappear before the kick-off into the crowd.

In the first ten minutes, England was in the ascendant, but the Welshmen stayed the distance better, and visions of a Cymric crack-up were dispelled, especially in the second half, when Wales were almost complete masters of the situation.

Wales had an excellent start, when Powell kicked an early goal from a mark. I remember lying on the ground to place the ball down, but the nonplussed Englishmen did not charge and the kick went over. We increased our lead to six points, when Jones-Davies scored a try, a masterly effort in which he bluffed Burland with a dummy and cut through between the English centres; though England's Bedford upset him he lifted the ball over the line, while still on the ground—quite legal.

After this, B. H. Black kicked a penalty goal to make it 6-3 to Wales. Then there came an extraordinary and strange incident, in which England scored five points. England made a sudden rally and a long kick found touch near the Welsh corner flag. Our unpredictable scrum-half, Powell, took on the duty of the Welsh wing at the throw-in. I was leading the Welsh pack, and ordered a short throw-in, but Powell threw a long ball to near the Welsh posts, in the expectation that the Welsh centres would take it; but Burland, the English centre, lying close up (no lying back ten yards rule then) caught the ball and ran in unopposed for a gift try. Both touch judges decided that Burland's kick for goal failed and the interval came with the score reading Wales 6 points, England 6; but the referee glanced at the score-board, and holding up eight fingers dramatically to the press-box indicated that he had overruled the touch-judges and awarded England a goal.

So at the restart Wales were two points behind. England were in the ascendancy for the first ten minutes, but feelings that Wales were not going to stay the distance were dispelled, and for the rest of the game they were complete masters of the situation. Jack Morley, our right wing, received the ball from Claude Davey (who had plunged through like a battering-ram) and cut into the middle of the field in his unorthodox fashion and crossed the line for a try, which Bassett converted.

So Wales, leading 11-8, seemed home and dry, but there was a dramatic climax. In literally the last minute of the game, Wales were penalised on the half-way line, five yards from touch; Black kicked a magnificent penalty goal for England, the game thus ending in a draw.

Would Wales ever win at Twickenham?

6 *The Bogey Slain*

In January 1933, on my fourth consecutive appearance for Wales at Twickenham, and as captain of the Welsh team, we had a nice blend of experience and youth, a fine side, which never played together again.

We had initiates to international rugby in Vivian Jenkins at full-back and nineteen-year-old Wilfred Wooller, from Colwyn Bay, in the centre. It could be said that this was the first truly representative Wales side, for we had in the second row Raymond Bark-Jones, captain of Cambridge University, also from North Wales, whereas previously Welsh representatives had come from South Wales. Ironically, England had in the back row a Welsh-speaking Welshman from South Wales in Vaughan Jones (The Army).

On the right wing we had Ronnie Boon (Cardiff), one of the best wings to play for Wales and of effervescent personality, definitely the man for the big occasion. In the centre was the experienced Claude Davey, who had played alongside Wilf Wooller for Sale, and fly-half Harry Bowcott (Cardiff and ex-Cambridge University), stylish and immaculate in all his play, his scrum-half partner being Maurice Turnbull, captain of Glamorgan County Cricket Club who died tragically on the beaches of Normandy.

In the forwards we had a seasoned front row in the all-Llanelli experienced trio of Edgar Jones and tireless bull-dog Archie Skym as props with Bryn Evans as hooker. Bryn broke his nose in the game after a quarter of an hour but refused to go off the field, such is the dedication of Welshmen to the Fatherland. I remember how his nose bled like a tap in the scrums. I was able to convey my orders to the front row in Welsh, no doubt much to the mystification of the English. Dai Thomas (Swansea) made up the second row, and with me in the back row were Tom Arthur, burly, good in line-out and loose, and Iorrie Isaacs, an open-side wing-forward, who subsequently played for Leeds in Rugby League as a centre, such was his all-round prowess.

The England team included Tom Brown (Bristol) as full-back, burly Don Burland (Bristol) as right centre, and Carl Aarvold on the left wing, captain of the side. The fly-half was Wally Elliot of the United Services. In the forwards were B. H. Black, our *bête noire* as a goal kicker, and Ray Longland (Northampton) as a prop, with Tony Roncoroni (Richmond) and Marine Charlie Webb, a great line-out forward, in the second row.

In my pre-game pep talk in the dressing-room, I did not tell my team, as reported in one English newspaper, 'If you see a dark object on the ground, kick it, it might be the ball; or tread on it, and if it squeals say "Sorry, old chap" and carry on.' What I did say, was for all to prepare to inure themselves to the constant Twickenham roar, rebounding on to the field from the stands, and to regard the game as a hotted-up version of a South Wales club-derby-game like Llanelli *v.* Swansea. The forwards were to heel from loose mauls, not to hack the ball as was the old tradition, and above all not to get offside; self discipline was essential. Iorrie Isaacs often related in after years how he silently prayed to God that England would not kick a penalty goal after he had fallen offside—this after my by no means soft-spoken admonition.

And so we went on to the field for the climax, the death of the Bogey. England should have scored twice in the opening twenty minutes when Burland broke through, but his openings were frittered away. It was then that, on the second occasion, I had a quiet fatherly talk with young Wooller, telling him to go low, which he did for the rest of the game, subduing Burland and getting off the mark now and again with a burst of speed and long stride. Claude Davey, his partner, was devastating, of course, in his tackling.

England had flouted providence but the Bogey was still alive. In twenty-five minutes, England went ahead by a controversial try when Booth, their wing, went racing for the line and passed inside to Elliot, who flung himself over the line when tackled, but the ball had been jerked out of his hands before he could touch it down. The referee awarded a try—maybe he was unsighted.

Gradually the game swung round with Wales getting on top, and at half-time I gave my team a pep talk on tactics. It was that with a following crosswind we were to get the ball back to Harry Bowcott, who would play the touch-line. Our forwards gave him the scope from scrum and line-out, where I did my share of providing. It all worked beautifully: when Bowcott got the ball he calmly and methodically measured his distance and banged it into touch within an inch or two of the point he had selected. It was as uncannily accurate as anything could be and it broke the spirit of the English side.

Within a minute of the opening half, Boon gave Wales the lead—fielding a loose ball and with plenty of time to do it he sent the ball high over the cross-bar with a drop kick well worth four points—a lovely thing to see. But the drama was not over. Bowcott's drop kick hit the posts and rebounded into play, then Wales knocked the ball back too vigorously and England fly-half Elliot snapped it up to dart off on his own, unmarked. A try seemed certain, the spectators rose to their feet and yelled, but when Elliot was within a few feet of the Welsh line Wooller the schoolboy came up like a racehorse, with long raking strides, and brought him down from behind. Welshmen mopped their foreheads, waved leeks and banged their saucepans.

England were never in the picture again, being pressed in their own twenty-five. There was a loose scrum, a quick heel by Wales, a pass by Davey with the defence out of position, and Boon ran around from the corner to score behind the posts for Wales to lead by 7-3. But there was considerable controversy after the score for Vivian Jenkins's conversion kick sailed at least a yard outside the goal-posts. The Welsh touch-judge put up his flag to indicate a goal, but the English touch-judge signalled that the kick had failed, and the referee did not blow his whistle. The score-board registered a goal to Wales, and this mistake was not corrected, so many spectators left the ground believing that Wales had won by six points, whereas they had won by four. But what did it matter? We took no more risks and when the final whistle went the Twickenham Bogey had been laid at last.

We celebrated, of course, and I remember one of our reserves telling me next morning that I was up rather early, when in fact I had just returned to our hotel at 6.45 a.m. The Welsh supporters had also celebrated, and I like the story told by a Ba-Ba of one of them who had also commemorated the victory and found himself late in the evening somewhat inebriated at Olympia watching the circus. 'Good old Wales, good old Wales,' he kept shouting vociferously, until he annoyed a gentleman sitting near with his family, who remarked, 'Excuse me, but would you mind stopping that noise, aren't you interested in the lions?' Turning round, the intoxicated Welshman shouted back, 'Lions! Lions! Watcyn Thomas would eat the bloody lot, man!'

Wales *v.* Scotland at Cardiff in 1931 I remember vividly because I was so involved personally and because of dramatic scores by Wales, who won by 13-8, the last score being one worthy of *Boys' Own Paper*. Wales fielded one of the strongest sides in which I played, with Jack Bassett, as full-back and captain, and Morley and Boon on the wings, the best pair to play for Wales since the days of Teddy Morgan and Llewellyn of the Welsh 'Golden Era'. In the centre we had Claude Davey, with Bowcott and Powell as half-backs. In the pack were the big and powerful Tom Arthur, Arthur Lemon, Ned Jenkins, Archie Skym, tireless as a dog, and Norman Fender (Cardiff), the best open-side forward then playing. As number eight, I led the Welsh pack on my seventh appearance for Wales.

In the backs, Scotland included the brilliant attacking pair of McPherson and Smith with scintillating Harry Lind at outside-half, an all-rounder good enough to play soccer in Scottish first division football. In the pack they had the amiable but not irresolute Mick Roughhead as hooker, supported by W. B. Welsh, Jock Beattie and first-cap Crighton-Miller.

The Welsh team assembled at the Esplanade Hotel, Penarth, before the game for lunch and tactical talks—not a procedure I agree with: a little enervating, I think, cooped up like chickens in a pen. It would have been a much better procedure for individual players to have made their way to a Cardiff hotel to dine and slip unobtrusively into the ground.

The pre-match tension was heightened when the coach conveying the Welsh team had the greatest difficulty in getting into the ground, another argument in favour of a Welsh Twickenham, which was to come later in the modernised and enlarged Cardiff Arms Park.

The gates closed before the kick-off; indeed, the game was started ahead of time to avoid trouble, and Wales scored before the advertised time of kick-off! Our scrum-half Powell sent on to fly-half Bowcott from a scrum and centre Davey drew the defence and handed to Morley, who ran with great determination to score in the right-hand corner in the first two minutes of the game amidst tumultuous cheering. Bassett failed to convert.

But the Scots were not dismayed and with ample possession from the scrums equalised. They swept down the field, and a cross-kick was taken on the wing by Wood, who raced up to Bassett and when tackled managed to get rid of the ball, Crighton-Miller following up to score a try. It was not converted, so the score was 3-3.

Half-time came, and as vice-captain and leader of the forwards I had to make a brave decision, even though personal feelings had to be hurt. Roughhead, the Scottish hooker, was having a field-day with the Welsh hooker clearly beaten. I switched our prop, T. Day of Swansea, to hooker and it worked. But before Wales could gain supremacy, Scotland scored again shortly after the kick-off. Lind broke away smartly and transferred to McPherson, who handed on to Crighton-Miller, who had no difficulty in scoring near the posts: what a début, scoring all Scotland's points but two, for Allen converted!

So Scotland were ahead 8-3; the honour of Wales was involved and so was I, '*Mae Hen Wlad Fy Nhadau Yn Anwyl i Mi*': 'The Land of My Fathers is Dear to me.' After Scotland had scored their second try shortly following the interval, I followed up the restarting kick, jumped, caught the ball, but was up-ended and fell on my left shoulder. I knew that I had broken my collar-bone but felt that if Wales were to play with a man short Scotland would take control and win, so I carried on leading the Welsh pack with my arm clasped to my chest. Wales hammered away outside the Scottish line for a long time, and after some inter-passing in the loose I was placed in possession of the ball ten yards out: I feinted to run to the right, stopped suddenly to catch the defenders on the wrong foot and moved to the left to charge over near the posts with a cluster of Scots hanging on to me. Our full-back Jack Bassett easily converted, so the score was eight points apiece. We continued to press and one minute from time Boon, the Welsh wing, drove the ball over the line to touch down for a try; when Bassett converted the whistle blew for time up. A fairy-story ending!

There was an astonishing sequel to the game. After my shoulder had been strapped up, I took my jersey into the Scottish dressing-room to exchange with one of the team (a time-honoured custom) but was ordered out by the stiff-necked Scottish official in charge, because it bordered on professionalism! However, there was a happy sequel, because the famous Scottish centre involved subsequently sent me his jersey, in secret through the postal service. Now, ironically, the Scots operate a squad-system and have national leagues. It's also noteworthy that one of the Scottish forwards, who played on the day, subsequently signed on and played for a Rugby League side, and so great was the disgrace that his name was erased from the honours board of the famous public school of which he was a former pupil.

Happily, there was the usual intermixing of both sets of players after the game, after which I retired to my hotel bedroom. But I did not sleep; I was in such pain that I paced my bedroom throughout the night, until I could travel back to St. Helens the next day. But it had been worth it for Wales went on to defeat Ireland and France and carry off the Championship.

I choose Scotland *v*. Wales in 1932 for special mention because it's the only international in which I played at Murrayfield, and what a magnificent stadium it is, though lacking the personality and intimacy of Twickenham and Cardiff Arms Park. But if the ground lacks character, which is indefinable, this is compensated by the aura emanating from the classical and noble Princes Street, and the wonderful war memorial on top of the mound. And above all there is the bountiful and lavish hospitality of the convivial and generous Scots.

Edinburgh has not been a happy hunting-ground for Wales and, perhaps, two stories will confirm my point. At Inverleith in 1924, the venue of Scottish international games, before Murrayfield was opened, Wales suffered a catastrophic and humiliating defeat by the staggering score of 10-35, Scotland scoring eight tries to two scored by Wales. Ian Smith, the Scottish right-wing, was in devastating form, and after the game at the dinner Tom Jones (Newport) called over the Welsh left-wing and said, 'Let me introduce you, I'm sure you two have not met before.'

On the following day, the Welsh team were taken by coach to see the Forth Bridge, where Jack Whitfield (Newport), one of the players in the débâcle, invited a fellow-international to have a good look at the Bridge, as he would never see it again at the expense of the Welsh Union.

Wales won the game in which I played by one try and a penalty goal to none. I did not realise that my name had been used by a Swansea rugger correspondent in the local evening newspaper in the few days prior to the game; a fictitious interview, giving my views on the Welsh prospects, whereas I was miles away in St. Helens. I joined the Welsh team at Crewe on the Friday and there was a pleasant re-union with my Welsh team colleagues, with Arthur Lemon insisting that Wales would win because the Welsh team mascot, 'Neddy'—a donkey —was tethered to the back of the train, and would bring us luck. We were a happy lot, all pals—so conducive to success on the field.

In Edinburgh we booked in and had a light training-session on the eve of the game, returning to our hotel for a bath on the second floor of our hotel, whereon to my astonishment a woman resident insisted on being transferred to another floor, because the Welsh team and reserves were running around naked in the corridor!

On the morning of the game I was taken with another

player to the local hospital to witness an operation on a woman patient for appendicitis, our host being a South Wales medical student who had failed on five occasions to qualify as a doctor. We were sitting in the gallery looking down upon the scene when I noticed that my player-friend had turned green and we left. It did not prevent my friend from making clinical tackles, for which he was famous, in the afternoon, when his opponent looked as green as he had in the morning.

I also had the pleasure of meeting in the foyer of our hotel that grand old war-horse, Jock Wemyss, surely descended from the ancient Greek Cyclops, who had played for Scotland in 1914 against Wales and Ireland, and for his country in 1920 and 1922 despite the fact that he had lost an eye in the 1914-18 war. With Jock was 'Teddy' Wakelam, ex-Harlequins captain, and precursor of all sound-radio broadcasts, his simulation in the lounge-bar of a broadcast by means of talking into an empty glass-tumbler sounding like the real thing.

Teddy was approached by one of the Welsh forwards, who asked him a favour, which was that when he mentioned the player's name would he please designate him not as from the first-class club for which he played, but as from the village in which he lived, as his mother, sisters and sweetheart were listening-in. Teddy was a great raconteur, and one of his stories was about a certain Army chaplain playing in an Army Cup Final at Aldershot; he dribbled the ball to an opponent, helping him off it with his boot in his posterior when he lay on it (fair enough, if you deliberately lie on the ball). The opponent involuntarily uttered a blasphemous ejaculation, whereupon the reverend gentleman, who had fallen on top of him, grasped him by the throat and said, 'Say sorry, you bastard!'

Wales were well supported, for 13,000 Welshmen travelled in thirty-six special trains to Edinburgh, the biggest band of excursionists sent to Scotland from the Principality for twenty years. Never had so many leeks and daffodils and red berets been seen in the venerable city, and the mound stand was like a poppy field. Wales fielded a very strong side, including Jack Bassett (Penarth) as full-back and captain, Boon (Cardiff) and

Morley (Newport) on the wings, with A. R. Ralph of Newport at fly-half and W. C. Powell (London Welsh) as scrum-half behind a powerful pack of forwards. Scotland played Ian Smith (London Scottish) on the wing and Harry Lind (Dunfermline) at fly-half, with W. B. Welsh (Hawick), J. W. Allan (Melrose), Mick Roughhead and F. H. Waters (both London Scottish) and Jock Beattie (Hawick) in the forwards. The two last named were two of the finest forwards to play for Scotland.

Scotland were beaten forward, again proving the axiom in rugby that beaten up in front, beaten everywhere, so Scotland, therefore, failed completely as an attacking force, and a Scottish raid rarely threatened danger as it wasn't often adequately supported, but a Welsh raid rarely failed for the lack of willing hands to help.

The referee overlooked too much offside work, and this led to trouble among the forwards. A considerable amount of unnecessarily provocative play and scrapping ensued, which culminated in a Scottish forward being hit under the jaw and knocked down. The ball was yards away at the time. Though the referee saw the whole incident the culprit escaped with a caution, and two minutes later was involved in another fracas. I'm pleased to say that, as leader of the Welsh forwards, I was able to stamp out this folly with a few stern words and was gratified after the game when the Welsh selectors thanked me in this respect. It's good to know that nowadays most referees take a sterner line and are also supported by the authorities for more draconian measures.

But back to the game itself. Wales scored after twenty minutes, after forcing the pace. Ralph made an admirable opening for Boon, who set off down the touch-line with thirty yards to go. He had only a few inches to spare, but he ran straight as a die, and his speed and resolution carried him over in the corner for a great try. Bassett failed to convert.

After the interval Wales attacked with persistent strength. The main virtue of the whole team was their excellent backing up in attack and covering in defence. Two of Scotland's individual efforts to score were foiled by Bassett's devastating tackles. Did he have the knack of hypnotising opponents into running into him? I rather think it was done by perfect positioning. That reminds me of Ernie Crawford, the old Irish full-back, who once told me that he talked to oncoming opponents, who became so bemused that they ran into his arms.

After twenty minutes of the second half Wales should have been credited with a try, when Morley kicked over the line, and outstripping his opposing wing by a yard touched down. The referee disallowed the try, but neither Morley nor ball went into touch-in-goal or over the dead-ball line. Spectators nearby, within a few feet of the spot, were flabbergasted as were all the Welsh players. Is this kind of thing a case in favour of touch-judges being able to run on to the field and advise referees on the validity or invalidity of scores, as is done in Association Football? The snag is that there would have to be a panel of neutral touch-judges and the loud cry of professionalism would be heard, but it's worth thinking about.

A Welsh score was bound to come: Powell found touch near the Scottish line. There was a scrummage, Wales heeled, and a Scot came round too eagerly and was penalised for being offside. Bassett took the kick from a wide angle and with a superb kick sent the ball high between the posts. There were not many minutes left and Wales ran out worthy winners.

Since Wales had defeated England at Swansea, they were well in line for winning the Triple Crown or the Championship at least, when playing Ireland in the next match at Cardiff. But the bounce of the ovoid ball has so often decided the result of a game and it played a great part in this. Towards the end, Wales were attacking and the Irish full-back had to run over his own line in order to save. His attempt to find touch from inside his own goal failed, the ball landing just short of the touch-line. With the line at his mercy, Morley the Welsh wing was beaten by the bounce and Lightfoot the Irish wing, who was palpably many yards offside, gathered the ball to race down the unguarded field to score a great try in the corner after running almost the length of the field, the try not being converted. Ireland were now leading by 12-7 but Wales pressed on and near the end scored a try through Ralph to make the score 12-10. Interest was now at fever-heat for conversion of the try would save the game for Wales by making it a draw, with the Championship going to Wales. Bassett took the responsibility of taking the kick but, alas, it failed and the whistle went for time up.

It was a chastening experience for Wales and chastening days were ahead of me, as I had to return to St. Helens the next day to be dragooned by my Headmaster.

The Prince of Wales is introduced to the Welsh team by Watcyn Thomas prior to the memorable 1933 game against England

England get the ball away from a scrum during the match they lost against Wales at
Twickenham

Watcyn Thomas, with a broken collarbone, scores the critical try against Scotland at Cardiff in 1931

The victorious Welsh team who defeated England at Twickenham in 1933. *Back row, left to right*, Bryn Evans, Vivian Jenkins, Wilfred Wooller, Iorwerth Isaacs, Tom Arthur, Dai Thomas; *middle row*, Arthur Jones, Raymond Bark-Jones, Ronnie Boon, Watcyn Thomas, Claude

8 *Waterloo Rugby Club*

During the time I taught at Cowley Grammar School in St. Helens, from 1929-37, I played for Waterloo Rugby Club and Lancashire, the happiest days of my rugby life.

At Cowley we taught on Saturday mornings, and on every Friday morning at recess a solemn rigmarole was played in the Headmaster's study. I would stand deferentially before his desk, after a bell had signified admittance, and humbly ask if I could be excused teaching during the last two lessons of Saturday morning, the time-table having been so arranged by a colleague that I was free. The martinet would ponder deeply and gravely and ask if I were free. Since the answer was in the affirmative, he would say, 'It's a mess Thomas, it's a mess, but you may absent yourself.' On my return to the staff-room I would be greeted by my colleagues with a chorus, 'It's a mess Thomas, it's a mess!'

The Waterloo pitch was, and still is, sandy, so that it drains well in the foulest weather. The stand and popular side are near and the ground gives you a cosy friendly feeling, so different from Murrayfield and many other renowned grounds, which are remote.

Waterloo was truly an amateur club, for players bought their own kit and jersey and paid their own travelling expenses to the ground. It was so amateur that no food was provided to players after the game, but jugs of beer or 'shandy' were available in the changing-room. No one limped into the bar after the game because of the florin stuffed into the toe of his shoe. It was the most sociable club I have known—committee, players and supporters moving freely without discrimination after the game.

This is more than can be said of a prominent first-class club in Birmingham, which on a big occasion reserved part of the clubhouse bar for the committee only. It took this club a long time to admit me at all, and on one occasion there I was refused admittance into the annexe-bar, the chief guests being an all-star side, but my being an ex-Barbarian Captain was of no avail. How different it was at Waterloo, which drew its players and members mainly from the middle-class.

Happy days at Waterloo, when on the field of play a shout of 'Hoi-hoi' meant you were up in support. We did not perform by set codes or numbers: set moves can be overdone and we relied on the innate genius of players. But we did have a pep-talk from the captain before the game. The skipper was a solicitor of engaging and disarming personality. He was once asked by a policeman in Liverpool on a Monday morning if he would not mind calling him a bastard on Saturday nights.

We had one or two characters in the team who were favourites with the tanner-bank spectators, the dockers of Birkenhead. What a contrast they were to most of the onlookers in the stand, where the club's president sat in eminence on a gilded throne. But I hasten to add that the Park Club players and committee were a grand lot, as were those of Sale R.F.C., which reminds me of the Waterloo player who, at Lime Street Station, Liverpool, asked a ticket collector, 'Is this train for Sale?' and on receiving a reply in the affirmative asked, 'Well, how much do you want for it?'

Noel Clint and I played for Lancashire on many occasions, and right royally we enjoyed ourselves on away games in the north against sides like Durham, Yorkshire, Cumberland and Northumberland. In the train dining-car on the way home we had a system whereby the restaurant car attendant, on hearing three rings of the bell-push, would bring us bottles of beer. The steward couldn't care less, since he was not paying, and a tip at the end of the journey satisfied him. I don't know what it cost the Lancashire Rugby Union on our long journey. One of Noel's favourite pranks in the dining-car was to blow up a preventive like a balloon and attach it to the air-conditioning fan at the door communicating with the rest of the train. It wafted in the airstream, and the downcast looks of the women who observed it gave him great cause for mirth. It's no wonder that the secretary of the Rugby Union told me years after, when I was resident at Ashby de la Zouch during the war and he a colonel, that the Lancashire players were regarded then as the wildest in the land.

Wild we were, certainly, but not vicious. I remember the occasion when Lancashire played on the Liverpool R.F.C. ground: beer was consumed in volumes in the bar of the club, after which we dined at a city club. Time went on and, since I had to return to St. Helens by train and it was rather late, I went down to the Club's basement to the toilet only to find the exit door locked. I gave the door a mighty heave, and it came away off its hinges in my hands. I stepped into the street outside, replaced the door as best I could and went on my way to catch the last train. At Waterloo the next Saturday, the Liverpool rugby secretary, who had booked the dinner, complained bitterly to me of the vandal's action, for the rugby club had to engage a night watchman to guard the premises. The secretary hastened to assure me that he knew I wouldn't have done such a dastardly deed. I didn't disillusion him; I never was a vandal.

But let us go back to the Waterloo Club, its environs, clubhouse and ground. It was a pleasure to walk to the ground from Blundellsands-Crosby railway station through a residential area. The clubhouse had tone without being ornate, and was not too big, so players and supporters were a happy family after the game. Clubhouses nowadays get bigger and bigger as commercial propositions, so that you get lost in the crowd and do not even meet close friends. At the beginning and end of a season, in good weather, after having changed and having consumed our fair share of ale, players and supporters would all kick a ball around and indulge in competitive games on the rugger-field. One I remember well. It was a challenge thrown out to the fastest players of the Club to overtake two men, one riding piggy-back on the back of the other, the player starting on the goal-line at our end of the field and the couple starting on the half-way line, the object being to reach the far goal-posts first. Surprisingly, the couple generally won, the only solo player I knew to win being the late Steve Meikle, our outside-half.

I played my first County Championship match for Lancashire against Cheshire in the season 1931-2, and in the next five years I was able to assist Lancashire in twenty-five matches, despite the claims of Welsh international games.

All that time I was making good rugby footballers of the boys at Cowley School, St. Helens. In the North, the Rugby League game has played an important part in the development of young Rugby Union players, whose lives are lived in the spheres of influence of the professional code. The youngsters of St. Helens, Wigan, Leigh and Barrow etc., where Rugby League flourishes, are afforded an opportunity to see how the game can be played by masters of their craft, and those lessons are not forgotten when they return to their school football and graduate to senior amateur rugby.

While I played up north, quite a few of the Lancashire side had been grounded in the more subtle arts of rugby by watching Rugby League as spectators—indeed I myself had learned a lot, and passed it on to my pupils. Prominent Lancashire players of my time included Jack Heaton (Waterloo and England), R. 'Dickie' Guest (Waterloo and England), first cousins incidentally and both natives of St. Helens, Roy Leyland (Waterloo and England), a native of Wigan and J. Bowker (Barrow). Jack Heaton was the finest exponent I have seen in this country of that very dangerous move, the grubber kick between opponents standing up closely in defence. The grubber-kick is performed by the exponent's toe and ball making contact on the ground simultaneously with the ball being propelled forward on the ground. It leaves opponents flat-footed, stranded and helpless. Jack Heaton in the centre and Dickie Guest on the wing were brilliant exponents of the scissors move just inside the touch-line. Heaton would deliberately run to the touch-line taking two opponents with him, and smartly turn to give an inside pass to Guest, who had cut in behind him, and the latter would be through unmarked. Both Guest and Heaton had a terrific side-step. Heaton would dip his hip and shoulders to left or right and then veer in the opposite direction, leaving opponents helpless. He is the best England centre I have seen. He could also kick goals and once against Cumberland scored six. He wasn't an individualist, though; he could and did make openings for others.

Both Guest and Heaton have been prominent members of the Lancashire Committee and set-up for some time. Dickie Guest's father was a great wit—his advice to me was never to be serious after 9 a.m. He was of the opinion, given to the Cowley Art Master, that the school scout-mistress of the cubs would be much happier sharing a tent with me when camping with her very young troop, and he once averred that a late tackle on me was so late that the match was over.

It's time we had a close look at the Lancashire team and personalities. The secretary was genial Tommy Bradburn and the treasurer was Eddie Stott. Bradburn was fanatically devoted to the success of the Lancashire side, and for some time acted as our touch-judge, until some of our players complained of his angry mutterings under the goal-posts when a try had been scored against us.

A popular member of the Lancashire side from time to time was 'Pop' Ogden of Fylde, a great character and wit. On one occasion we were playing Yorkshire away at Bradford, and as our coach drew up outside the ground a band was playing, so 'Pop' leaned out of the window and asked, 'Excuse me, can you play the refrain from spitting?' 'Pop' was a highly skilled and successful goal-kicker, but his method was most unorthodox, for he used to kick goals not with toe or instep but with the side of his foot.

Another popular member of the side was H. B. (Bert) Toft, later to captain England. His monologues, including 'Albert and the Lion' and others, were hilarious. A man who played for Lancashire at this time was G. P. Vallance (Leics), who was chosen to play for England but had to drop out because of a heavy cold and was never selected again. But his experience was not so mortifying as that which happened to a chosen England player in the 1920s: he was actually photographed as a member of the England team before the kick-off, and then ordered to stand down by the selection committee as they considered that the weather conditions that had set in were too wet for him.

Weather conditions remind me of the occasion when Lancashire were due to play East Midlands at Northampton in 1933 in the semi-finals of the County Championship. It was one of winter's cold spells and grounds were frozen hard, but the Lancashire and East Midlands Committee were conned by a plausible fellow who convinced them that he had invented an anti-freeze liquid which, when sprayed on the field, would instantaneously defrost the ground. When we arrived on the ground we found that the antidote had aggravated the conditions and we all skated on the parts of the ground where the 'cure' had been applied.

The game had to be played the following week, but we had our fun on this frozen occasion. We retired to the local Conservative Club as the guests of the late Edgar Morgan, one of the Welsh 'terrible eight' of 1914. In the bar I noticed a series of undulating movements in a sack lying on the floor, and when the sack was untied we extracted a live cockerel. I released the bird into the street outside, where we had a gay time catching it, bets being laid on its recapture. I was not successful, and had the task of mollifying the returned owner, the provision of a few pints doing the trick.

The Lancashire side were a lively lot certainly, so on to players and reserves from whom a typical Lancashire side was chosen in those days, and a notable game, in which I played, leading up to the climax, when Lancs won the County Championship for the first time: F. B. R. Horne (Furness); three-quarters from A. Craven and R. D. Cotton (both Fylde), J. Heaton (Waterloo and England), Roy Leyland (Liverpool University, Waterloo and England), Claude Davey (Sale and Wales), Ian Calder (Waterloo), Eric Gore (Liverpool University), E. S. Estcourt (Fylde), R. Guest (Liverpool University, Waterloo and England), G. W. C. Meikle (Waterloo and England). Outside half-backs: G. S. C. Meikle (Waterloo and England) and T. Bowker (Furness); inside: J. B. McArthur (Waterloo and Scotland) and J. C. Pank (Furness). Forwards from W. H. Leather (Liverpool), H. B. Toft (Broughton Park, Waterloo and England), J. A. Cooper (Warrington), G. P. C. Vallance (Leics), G. W. Whelpton (Vale of Lune and the Army), Watcyn Thomas (Waterloo and Wales), H. C. Fry (Liverpool and England), J. Mycock (Sale and England), N. Clint (Waterloo), J. Chubb (Waterloo).

It will be noticed that eleven of the above played for their country at some time or other, but the weakness was that they were a cross-section of eight different clubs, so that cohesion in vital games was not always possible, individual brilliance by some having to suffice, with the rest slogging it out. The success of Warwickshire in the County Championship in recent years has been based on the fact that the side has been composed mainly of players drawn from the Coventry, Rugby and Nuneaton sides, the Coventry players being preponderant. Gloucestershire has been in the same happy position.

This lack of team work was sadly illustrated when Lancashire played East Midlands in the county semi-final at Waterloo in February 1934, when Lancs lost by 18-19, after leading at half-time by 15-0. The Lancs backs had not played together for two months, and it should be pointed out that that interval between the last group games and the semi-final was a much greater handicap to counties, which chose their sides from many clubs, than to those who drew from only two or three. No two men playing side by side in any part of the Lancs side had had that association in club matches, whereas the East Midlands pack was all Northampton except for the

Lancashire's 14-0 win over Somerset at Bath in June 1935 gave them the County Championship for the first time since 1891. *Above*, a scene from the match; *below*, G. W. C. Meikle, D. M. H. Craven, G. P. C. Vallance, Watcyn Thomas, J. Mycock, W. H. Leather, W. J. Leather; *seated*, R. Horne, R. Leyland, J. Heaton, T. J. Bradburn (hon. secretary), H. B. Toft, H. A. Fry, J. A. Cooper; *front*, J. Bowker, L. Swann

Above, Watcyn Thomas is given an affectionate send-off on his retirement from the teaching staff at King Edward Grammar School, Aston; *below*, reunion at London-Welsh Rugby Club; *left to right*, Watcyn Thomas, Wilfred Wooller, Harry Bowcott, Raymond Bark-Jones and Tom Arthur hooker. The Mids halves, Gadney and Slow, were a Leicester Club pair, while wings Treen and Chorlton also formed a club pair.

The defeat at Waterloo was a sad blow for Lancashire, who, season after season, were so near and yet so far. It must have been almost unprecedented for a county to reach the semi-finals five times in six seasons and thrice to go through to the final stage without gaining the ultimate honour of winning the Championship. The Lancs defeat was the result of the East Midlands team work, the latter fighting a gallant up-hill battle and turning what seemed sure defeat into a dramatic and deserved success. Dramatic it certainly was: in the last two minutes with a scrummage in front of the Lancs posts B. C. Gadney spoke to his fly-half Slow, and in the next second the ball was heeled and Slow dropped the ball over the bar for four points to make the score 19-18 in E. Midlands favour. That was the finish though the formality of restarting the game was gone through for half a minute.

It is interesting to note that E. Mids also included J. E. Tallant (Blackheath), that grand old war-horse Ray Longland and A. D. Matthews in the pack. Austin Matthews and I both sustained cut eyes and went to a local doctor after the game to have them stitched, after which we returned to the club-house to fraternise in the usual fashion. Austin Matthews was a most unlucky player as far as international honours were concerned. He would have been a great asset as a forward to the Welsh XV, but had to deputise on the wing for most of the game in a Welsh trial and was not chosen for the next and last trial—truly the minds of the Welsh selectors in those days were unfathomable.

Since I had reshuffled the Welsh team on the field at Dublin in 1933, against the wishes of the Welsh selectors, it isn't surprising that I was not chosen for Wales in 1934, so I hope I shall be excused for a personal 'puff' relating to the semi-final described above. In 1933, the accurate pin-point kicking of Harry Bowcott into touch under my orders won the game for Wales. But in this semi-final the Lancs backs kept kicking into the open, which ended in the visiting backs pumping the ball into touch near the Lancs line.

I quote a Lancashire rugby correspondent of the day: 'The results of the unfavourable kicking duels began to tell territorially but the Lancashire pack never lost its cohesion. To single out one forward, where all did so well, including Harry Fry and Joe Mycock, may seem ungracious, but I am sure the forwards will have no objection to my rewarding the honours of the match to Watcyn Thomas. The famous Welshman is accused sometimes of taking a game easily, but how many forwards can go all out every time they play, and hope to be on top of their form month after month? I have seen Watcyn Thomas loitering in some matches this season, but I have seen him playing many magnificent games, notably against Durham, Dublin Wanderers and East Midlands, and on his play in the last mentioned he must be considered one of the best three forwards in the home unions today.' My comment on the above is that 'loitering' means keeping an eye open in defence and attack, conserving energy and applying it at the right moment, and knowing by instinct where to be in attendance the next second. Splendid illustrations of this flair are Dave Morris (Wales) and Mervyn Davies (Wales) and it was illustrated in my case when the late W. G. Davies wrote in a London paper re a Lancs *v*. East Mids semi-final game at Northampton in 1933 which Lancs won in the snow by 16-10, 'Watcyn Thomas was superb for Lancs: he never seemed to be out of trot, but he was always at the right spot at the right moment and his saving was invaluable.' You cannot cultivate or buy instinct. You are born with it.

I played for Wales against South Africa at Swansea on Saturday, December 5th, 1931, when the tourists won by 8-3. The Wales captain was Jack Bassett, playing as full-back, and before him there lined up backs capable of winning any international in J. C. Morley and Claude Davey on the right flank of the three-quarters with Ronnie Boon on the left wing and Frank Williams as his centre. Our scrum-half was W. C. Powell and our outside-half R. Ralph. Wales had powerful forwards in Tom Arthur, 'Ned' Jenkins, Arthur Lemon, Archie Skym, Will Davies and myself. The South African full-back was G. Brand and the half-backs playing before him were Danny Craven as scrum-half and Benny Osler as fly-half and captain. The South African hooker was the veteran Phil Mostert with the giants Daneel and 'Boy' Louw packing behind him in the second row. The game was played in torrential rain throughout with Lady Luck deciding the outcome.

It is not true, as stated by some, that no English was spoken on the field; but it is true that the South African forwards spoke Afrikaans, and that many of the Welsh forwards, including myself, who was pack leader, spoke Welsh or understood it, so that among the forwards at least there could be no interpretation of the opponents' intents.

It's interesting to note that some press correspondents referred to the Springboks as the 'Colonials' (shades of the Boer War!). The forwards on both sides were some of the finest physical specimens ever to play rugby—not strange in the case of men reared on the Veldt, but remarkable in the case of the Welshmen and a tribute to the resilience of the Welsh throughout the Industrial Revolution, the natural law of the survival of the fittest operating. In contrast to the Veldt dwellers, the Welsh front row of Archie Skym, A. F. 'Lonser' Bowdler and Tom Day were practising or ex-coalminers, with Will Davies our wing-forward, then currently a collier.

The result on the field was a titanic struggle among the forwards, climatic conditions deciding the tactics and the outcome, the adventitious element of luck being the predominant factor in winning or losing. On a dry day I think Wales with a galaxy of stars in the backs would have won, but who can tell? We played on a quagmire and in a rain-storm, and Benny Osler, the South African fly-half and captain proved himself a master tactician: he adapted himself and his side to the conditions by kicking the ball into touch at every possible moment. He had already gained for himself in Wales the pseudonym of 'Willie Kick', or 'Benny Kick'. It must be remembered that in those days there were no restrictions on kicking into touch in any part of the field. He had an excellent scrum-half in Danny Craven, subsequently to be known as 'Mr. Rugby'.

I have said weather conditions decided the result of the game, and any side could have won. After a bright early morning, the God of Rain intervened. Before noon, heavy rain began to descend steadily and it continued throughout the afternoon for the whole of the game without intermission.

The rain had its effect on the crowd, estimated at 40,000 at the kick-off. The stands were full, but there was plenty of room on the cheap side, 'the tanner bank'. The Springbok mode of play on their Welsh tour, forward domination and kicking to touch was alien to Welsh tradition and method of play, and there was a curious lack of verve and enthusiasm for a Welsh crowd. There were no troupes of scarlet-bereted followers, no monster leeks and colourful red rosettes. An hour before the kick-off, when *Sospan Fach* and Welsh hymns are normally sung with full voice and emotion, the atmosphere was dumb and dismal, without the usual badinage.

No one tried to fix a leek to the uprights and as the rain cascaded down, ring-side seat-holders used newspapers, sacking or any kind of improvised cover. A quarter of an hour before the start the light was so bad that press men had to rely upon electric light from adjacent telephone cubicles to write their introduction to their reports. Perhaps this general state of affairs was one of the factors much later on in time that convinced the Welsh Rugby Union that Cardiff should be the only venue for rugby international games. The game began on a sea of mud, and it was certain there would be few orthodox movements in the match. The obvious thing to do was to kick and rush with the forwards bearing the brunt of the fight, indeed, all the tries were scored from fly-kicks, and fast following up. Oddly enough, in such conditions, there was no ill-feeling, even though players who were brave enough to go down to the ball were helped off it unceremoniously. There was one light-hearted incident when a Springbok enquired, 'Why for you kick me?' and received the reply 'It's in case you start something'—this from Arthur Lemon, great wit, and not the culprit. Tackling was exceptionally keen, and whenever a player was held at close quarters he was buried deep in mud; the players were literally coated with mud from head to foot, shipping eyes full of mud and having to be sponged and towelled.

In the first half the Welsh team were the better, and after twenty minutes scored. Welsh wing Boon fly-kicked up the field, the Springbok full-back tried hard to recover but failed in the awful conditions and Will Davies, the Welsh wing-forward, dribbled on to score a try for Wales. This was the first try scored by Wales against South Africa in the long history of their encounters—you can do something for the first time once only, so all honour to Davies, nicknamed 'Skeely', to differentiate him from the legion of other Davieses I suppose.

Bassett failed to convert but five minutes from half-time Wales should have been credited with another try to give them a six-point lead. Davey and Morley went away with the ball at their feet: Morley drove the ball past Brand, the South African full-back, five yards over the line, fell on it and touched down before slithering into touch, but the referee, left hopelessly in the rear, disallowed the score.

In the second half, the Springboks adapted themselves well to the conditions—could it have been Cape Province winter weather? But it was certainly not warm and wet as school geography text-books describe a Mediterranean type of climate, though wet it certainly was. Play was scrappier than ever, and it must have been comical for some spectators to see both sets of players fly-kick the ball, which remained almost stationary. Benny Osler, the South African captain, did not contribute a great deal of note, but he won the match by his insistence on the absence of passing, and that his forwards should keep kicking and hacking hard forward, trusting to the Welsh defence making mistakes—good captaincy and it paid off, for their footwork caused the Welsh backs considerable trouble. The Welsh backs on the other hand kept persistently to a policy of hand-passing, trying to keep the game open—folly as the ball was as slippery as a piece of ice. Handling by the Welsh backs broke down and Danny Craven kicked forward a high ball, which Morley tried to mark but failed to gather, and Daneel the Springbok forward sent the ball over the line to touch down in a favourable position for a conversion, but Brand, hero of so many miraculous place kicks on the tour, failed to convert, sending the ball barely ten yards along the ground. A Welsh centre appealed to the referee that he had grounded the ball before Daneel scored, and a supporter ran on to the field to expostulate and support the claim but he was hustled off by a policeman—such spectator conduct was un-heard of in those days!

Play continued and the Springbok forwards broke away in a dribble, one of them driving the ball through the Welsh full-back Bassett's legs (such were the conditions) five yards from the line; Bergh hacked the ball over the line to score a try in a splendid position for a conversion. Osler converted so South Africa were nearly home but not dry, leading by 8-3. They hung on grimly to their lead; as it came to them from Welsh forays, which were now frequent, and deserving of a score, they kicked the ball in any direction away from their line and tackled like men possessed, leaving the field heroes and winners of an epic struggle.

Who knows if the 'Boks' would have won in different weather conditions, but they could certainly play well in dry weather as they proved on the following Tuesday when they trounced a combined Lancashire and Cheshire side at Waterloo. I played for the mixed Northern side, and hope I shall not be considered conceited if I quote this excerpt from the *Manchester Guardian* report: 'Few who saw the game will forget it. Time after time Watcyn Thomas threw the ball to his backs, until at each line-out he was almost surrounded by opponents. The ball would be thrown in, there would be an immense upheaval in the middle of the ring, and just as the ring fell to the ground, back would come the ball. Completely buried under a pile of opponents, Watcyn Thomas would be released, entirely unscathed, wearing on his face the characteristic and habitual expression of complete indifference.' I wonder why, nowadays, so many forwards in the line-out knock the ball backwards or forwards with one hand.

During the period I played for Waterloo, Lancashire and Swansea (on vacations), I also had the privilege of playing for the Barbarians on several occasions, and the honour of being captain of the sides against Leicester and Swansea. The method of selecting the personnel of the famous touring side was a mystery to me, but I do know that the Club had capable, experienced rugger men at the helm, who took the advice and opinion of seasoned players on the suitability of current players to be chosen for the honour of playing. I remember I was able to advocate the inclusion of Jack Heaton and Roy Leyland of Lancs in the side.

The officials of the Club in my playing days were rugger men to the core, with playing and administrative experience. The Secretary was Haigh Smith, dour in manner but a perfect gentleman. The president in my time was lovable Emile de Sissa, and the treasurer D. T. Glynn Hughes, who, later on, was for a considerable time the Club's president. 'Hughie' made a remarkable return to the Forces during the last war, ending up as a prominent 'brass-hat'. A notable attendant figure on the Welsh Easter tour was Jock Wemyss of Scotland, who lived for rugby football.

The qualification for being selected for the Ba-bas was that you had to be a good player of gentlemanly behaviour. I qualified as a good player, since I had played for Wales, and had impressed when playing for Swansea against the Barbarians on their Easter tour. Swansea used to win the encounter generally, team-work triumphing over a bunch of star players, thrown together for one game. Perhaps the fact that I scored a try for Swansea against them helped to get me an invitation to play for the tourists. The try was scored in the cheekiest manner imaginable. The Barbarian scrum-half decided to break from the scrum under their posts with ball in both hands and waving it in the air to nonplus his opponents, but I snatched the ball out of his hands and walked two paces forward to score a try under the posts! A conversion gave us a great win.

The personnel of the touring side in my day was a good mixture of English, Welsh, Scottish and Irish internationals, the last mentioned being as exuberant as ever, on one occasion reducing the assembled tourists at the hotel dinner to silence by singing *The Soldiers' Song* after our national anthem.

The hotel at which we stayed on the South Wales tour was the Esplanade, Penarth, under the tolerant, understanding and indulgent proprietors Mr. and Mrs. King. The chief waitress and major-domo combined was Peggy, who catered to our needs even into the small hours of the morning. There were high-jinks at night at the hotel, but there was a standing rule that players engaged in a game the next day had to retire to bed at 11 p.m. For some reason or other I was excused this restriction: perhaps it was because of my known capacity for holding my pints, which I drank galore without getting intoxicated— a triumph of mind over matter! Alas, I have not the same resilience now.

There was the added physical factor that at Easter I would play as many as five games in six days, and beer helped to replace body salts lost and prevent staleness. After galloping around for the first fifteen minutes the beer residue had been sweated out, and I was as fit and fresh as a daisy. This 'training' at Easter would not have suited everyone: some players liked a sherry before a game 'to help the wind', but I never drank alcohol before a match. Many players are teetotal and play superbly—it's all a matter of metabolism and fitness.

To be fit a player must train hard. I trained rigorously for my games, and accordingly enjoyed them—unfit and stale players tend to arrive at the location of the ball late, enough to make the difference between success and failure, enjoyment and hard labour. I trained hard twice a week until the sweat poured off me, with road-work sometimes interspersed. I remember training on one occasion at Llanelli, doing field and road-work at midnight, when I was pulled up by a policeman, nicknamed 'Tom Pen Taten' (Tom Potato Head), but I was able to reassure him that my activity wasn't nefarious.

But let me hark back to the Ba-bas. The team certainly enjoyed itself at Penarth and there was a good deal of high jinks at the Esplanade Hotel after our game and evening meal. Beer was drunk out of bottles extracted from laid-out cases, there being a gentleman's agreement that a chit should be signed for each number of bottles extracted. If we were hungry, we cooked our own meals of bacon and eggs, and duly signed for them.

Newly joined Ba-bas were initiated into the mysteries of the club by ordeal by fire and water, with myself the chief priest clad in head-towel and a bed-sheet, *à la* Ku-Klux-Klan. For fire worship, the carpets were rolled back and newspapers lighted, while the novices and full members danced around the bonfire like dervishes, howling incantations and ending up on their knees facing Mecca. The initiates then underwent ordeal by water, being thoroughly soused by buckets of water thrown over them, but not before their shirts were ceremoniously burned. Great was the chagrin of one of the pillars of the Ba-bas to find that to make the ceremony more impressive his costly silk shirt, purloined from his bedroom, had been burnt.

Prior to these high jinks, we all, on Saturdays, attended the local dance hall, where on one occasion and for some strange reason, some of us were refused admission. Access was gained by our climbing up the exterior wall spouting on to the outside balcony of the hall, which we entered to make a ceremonious entry on to the dance floor by leaping from the gallery on to the chandeliers and dropping down below, where we behaved with decorum.

Our return to the hotel was not so sedate and decorous. Accompanied by another player I knocked off the helmet of a policeman, who pursued us hot-foot to our hotel, while we indulged in inter-passing with the helmet. The policeman turned out to be Morgan Hopkins of the Glamorgan Police XV, who bearing us no animosity and in typical rugby camaraderie joined us in a few pints of beer.

Success at last! Lancashire won the County Championship in 1935, for the first time since 1891, by defeating Somerset in the final at Bath by a goal and three tries to nothing, a convincing win by 14-0. Success was long overdue, since Lancs at this time had reached the semi-final five times in six seasons, and thrice had gone through to the final stage without gaining the ultimate honour.

The game was not as torrid or as grim as others in which I had played in the County Championship, the semi-final at Coventry against Warwickshire having been much harder. The Lancashire side was in a class above that of its opponents. In mid-field we had Jack Heaton and Roy Leyland, both of Waterloo in the centre, playing behind J. Bowker (Furness) as fly-half and J. C. Pank (Furness) as scrum-half. How useful to have a club pair as half-backs. Readers, no doubt, will recollect many famous club combinations, who played for their country in international games. Our hooker was H. B. Toft and the back row was composed of Harry Fry (Liverpool) as open-side wing-forward, and Joe Mycock (Sale) as blind-side wing-forward, with myself as No. 8 in the middle of the back row. Apart from the half-backs, all these attained or were to attain international status, and Toft, Heaton, Mycock and myself at some time or other were captain of their national sides.

Roy Leyland, with his snipe-like zig-zag runs, was the perfect foil to Heaton, and he had been instrumental in our winning the semi-final at Coventry, when he ran from his own 25 to score under the posts towards the end of the game. Harry Fry was a superb open-side wing-forward and could play like a man possessed. Of his play in a previous county game a rugby correspondent had written, 'He seemed willing to play the whole Cumberland side himself.' Joe Mycock had played for Lancashire first at the age of seventeen, and he, Fry and myself had a perfect understanding on how to seal off the mid-field in defence, and we were always at hand in attack. Mycock was also a fine line-out forward.

Bath was a sedate town, rather more sedate than Newcastle, where on two visits there with Lancashire I was greeted out-side our Railway Hotel by a vendor of newspapers with a strident cry of *Evening Echo* (or equivalent) and a sotto-voce follow-up of, 'French letters two shillings a box.' Nothing like that could have happened in Bath, but I fear that after our post-game dinner and celebrations we scandalized the sedate natives and resident visitors, for outside our hotel next morning—a Sunday at that—there hung chamber-pots from flag poles and bedroom windows. These were not gestures that we had 'hissed' over our opponents, but just another manifestation of our team's high spirits. Letters of protest were printed in the local, regional and London newspapers, but by then I was far away, home and dry, in the quiet confines of cloister and classroom. I was most indignant and hurt when my head-master in his study asked me if I had been involved in the frolics—as if I, a Welsh Baptist, could have been guilty of such a thing.

Back to the match: there was a 12,000 crowd—the biggest that had attended a rugby game in Somerset. We arrived on the ground sedately enough, each wearing a red rose, the badge of the Lancastrians in the Wars of the Roses, but the game itself, I fear, was no battle—we were too good. In the first half there was nearly forty scrums, which shows how the rugby game has been tidied up since my playing days. The first half was colourless and fairly even, but in the second half we were well on top thanks to our concerted shove at the put-in and Toft's hooking, and the heeling was 3-1 in Lancashire's favour. And, to quote a report on the game, 'as the Lancs work in the line-out was better than any done by a northern side for years, it is not surprising that Somerset became a much harassed side.' We had possession and attacking ability and flair as shown when our wing Craven scored Lancs third try—a spread-eagled defence, lightning speed of execution and a final dive over the line. Heaton scored Lancashire's fourth try in a typical effort in which he sidestepped three men and threw himself over between two of his opponents.

And so we brought home the bacon, but not all the glory belonged to the backs: forwards lay the foundations of victory, so I may be excused a puff for quoting a newspaper rugby correspondent of the time: 'Watcyn Thomas was a great man in an excellent pack of forwards, who laid the foundations of victory. He never seemed to require a "breather", but worked tremendously hard in every minute. He lived up to his reputation as an artist in the line-out, and used his weight in the set scrums; he was quick in getting into position for loose mauls, and was always ready to assist in attacks or defence. His seven colleagues followed his example.'

I hope the account of my method of play will be of use to present-day back-row forwards.

In January 1937, after my sojourn at St. Helens, I began teaching at King Edward VI Grammar School, Aston, Birmingham, where I remained in harness until July 1971, a period of thirty-four years. Happy days in a school of about three hundred and fifty boys and approximately thirty masters, under the tutelage of Leonard Brandon as headmaster and Frank Bentley as second master, grand men, who let the staff get on with their job without dragooning or prying.

Most of the staff were middle-aged and amicable: there were no coteries or cliques; of course, all had nicknames, my own inevitably being 'Taffy'. The Chairman of the staffroom was Hothersall, known to the boys as 'Hairy', a nickname acquired because of his hairy legs peeping out from behind his desk. The head of the English department was George Painter, erudite and sensible, who on his retirement returned to the school for part-time teaching. He was slightly deaf and the boys had learned to mouth their answers without speaking, causing George to think that his hearing-aid had broken down. The head of the Geography department was Freddie Ball, nicknamed 'Jimmy Pill'. Houses were named after senior masters and he turned down the honour of becoming a house-master owing to the possible rallying cry on the school playing-field at inter-house rugger matches of 'Come on Ball's!'

One house-master was Arthur Smith, the finest French teacher in England, since H.M. Inspectors used to visit the school to watch and hear him teach. Hear him they certainly did, since he was somewhat deaf and had evolved a system in class by which the knowledgeable boys in answering questions jumped up like a Jack-in-the-box and shouted their answers at the tops of their voices. With a sliding scale, the chosen, successful boys moved to the back of the class, while the failures moved down to the front row, a kind of mug's alley. These were detained after school, when they were made to climb in and out of classroom windows on to the abutting school yard for one hour, or run up and down the school staircase or climb ladders, if available, for the same period of time.

Another house-master was Bill Mayers, nicknamed 'Buggy', a stickler for etiquette and somewhat humourless sober-minded Welsh nationalist. One day he was refereeing a rugger match in which the 1st XV were playing a day-continuation school, an unruly, ill-disciplined lot, who kept querying his decisions. Bill got paler and paler but it was the ultimate indignity when the visiting captain at the end of the game went to him to apologise with the words: 'I'm sorry Sir, but it's these bloody Welshmen we've got in the side.'

One of our house-masters was the laziest schoolmaster I knew. He came into the staffroom one day with the information that a class was unsupervised and playing hell; could they be invigilated he asked—it was his own class and he promptly sat down to read the newspaper, while a junior member of the staff retired to take over. He was fond of secluding himself in the toilets during teaching periods, from which he was hauled out more than once by the headmaster. He was the self-appointed third master and one day when taking prayers convulsed the whole school-assembly by breaking wind resoundingly in the middle of his peroration. He once asked our wood-work master to make him a wooden cross, since he wished to present it to his church, of which he was an elder. The wood-work master obliged, but it was at the school's expense. He was fond of taking time off for days and I once met him in the street on one of his 'holidays', when he dramatically flourished a card, which informed me that he was forbidden to speak by his doctor, as he had lost his voice. Why he could not have invigilated classes in school I don't know. When he paid a visit on a social call he would stay for two hours, but

I solved this by peeping through the front-room curtain and not answering the bell of the door.

There were other interesting characters on the staff including the art master, who eventually became an A.R.A. and who got married in a free period, and lovable Billy Lumb, who taught French and German. He was very much like a music-hall character with his favourite expression, 'I say old chap, old chap, what!' He had a temper which flared up instantaneously and died down as suddenly. So quick-tempered was he that on one occasion during the war, when the school housed another school and staff, he tipped a rice-pudding over the head of an unfortunate guest-master in the dining-room. He once re-marked to me that a certain boy was a queer fellow, since in the middle of a lesson he had piped up with the question 'Excuse me Sir, how much did you pay for your gold watch, and where did you buy it?' He could not see that he was being ragged, but so well-beloved was he that when he retired the Old Boys and I gave him a great send off in a town hostelry. At the end of our night out Bill discovered that his hat had been stolen; being bald he overcame the problem and the cold by buying hot pork pies from a street vendor and clapping them to his head until his bus arrived!

One of the greatest characters in the school was our care-taker, Charles Hudson, known to all the boys as 'Chaz'. He knew every boy in the school by name and his home back-ground. 'Hudsonisms', like malapropisms, were famous, 'multiciple bank' for Municipal bank being one of them. One day he entered the staffroom and said to me 'Excuse me Sir, a would-be parent wishes to see you.' It was the mother of a new boy, who was joining the school the next day. I was sorry that I could not oblige her. 'Chaz' was a good-hearted soul, who had been at the school for many years, and left this earth as he probably would have wished by dying suddenly in the school lodge in the morning of the last day of term. I, as a teacher of first-aid, had the melancholy task of pronouncing life extinct.

We had characters among the pupils as well, not all of them

savoury. Two of them, brothers, engaged themselves in stealing from the cloakrooms from the very first day they entered the school. They ended up in Dublin gaol for bank robberies, from which prison they one day escaped. The younger was recaptured immediately, but the elder evaded arrest for some time while he hopped from one place to another in England. Nemesis eventually overtook him, however, and he was retaken.

But let us end up on a lighter note. The boys in the school were an honest lot, cheerful, good-hearted and willing to take their gruel without rancour. The only occasion on which I was in real trouble was when an irate mother came to school to complain to the headmaster about my method of discipline of gentle taps. But all ended well at the end of the interview in the Head's study with the mother's parting words, 'And Mr. Taffy, next time give him a bloody good clout for me.'

A Poor Evacuee at Ashby de la Zouch

Two days before the outbreak of war in September 1939, King Edward VI Grammar School was evacuated to Ashby de la Zouch, Leicestershire, a small market town seventeen miles west of Leicester with a population of a little over 4,000. There I dwelt until after the end of the war, when the school returned to Aston.

Ashby has a distinguished pedigree, being a very old township in origin. The name first occurs in the Domesday Book, in which the name is spelt 'Ascebi', then in the reign of Edward VI (1547-53), when the King Edward Schools were founded, a survey of church property quoted it as 'Ashebiedela—Souche'. The Anglo-Saxon form of the word 'ash' was 'aesc', to which was added the Danish word 'by' meaning abode, and three French words 'de la Zouch', the whole meaning 'the dwelling place by the ash tree of the Zouch'. The French connection was acquired by the fact that about 1130 the daughter of the Lord of the Manor married Alan la Zouch, a descendant of the Earls of Brittany, and he thus became Lord of the Manor. Without modesty he called it Ashby de la Zouch to distinguish it from numerous other Ashbys in the Midlands.

Apart from its ancient traditions, the town has modern historical associations. Dominating the approach from the Birmingham side is an Eleanor Cross, 70 ft. high and designed by Sir Gilbert Scott to commemorate the memory of the Countess of Loudoun (1833-74), noted for her good works among the poor of Ashby. This form of cross was so named from the crosses Edward I (1272-1307) erected to mark the places where the body of his Queen, Eleanor (*d.* 1290), rested on its journey to Westminster. The Ashby Cross was unveiled on July 24th, 1879.

At the other extreme and northern end of the town is the castle, first mentioned between 1128-1149, but of this castle only a few traces now remain. This is the castle mentioned in *Ivanhoe* as the scene of Prince John's revels, the date being about 1194. The present ruins are those of the second castle built by William, Lord Hastings, about 1494.

A propos *Ivanhoe*, there is no other place in the vicinity of Ashby that corresponds to Sir Walter Scott's description of the Tournament Fields as the fields west of the road between the town and the neighbouring village of Smisby. To be less sublime but still historical, there stands near Smisby Church an ancient 'House of Correction', in which drunks and thieves were locked up. In shape it resembles a candle-extinguisher.

I never saw a drunk in Ashby but there are plenty of hotels, old inns and pubs in the town. Near the Eleanor Cross is the Royal Hotel with a portico perhaps disproportionately large. At its rear is the Pump House of the old Spa, Ashby at one time being a fashionable watering-place. The water was carried from outlying villages. The George Hotel in the main street, Market Street, evidently dates from the time of the Hanoverian Dynasty, whom it has easily outlived. In Market Street just below the Market Hall is the inn quaintly known as The Hole In the Wall, situated at the end of a narrow passage. It had the great advantage in my time that prominent and respectable business men and schoolmasters could dive into it unseen if they made quick sidesteps. Some would have won great acclaim at Twickenham or Cardiff Arms Park. On the opposite side to the Hole In The Wall is the Bull's Head, which seems to be the oldest house in the town. It was the resort of the Parliamentarians during The Commonwealth, and there is a tradition that Oliver Cromwell lodged there. I will not equate myself with the Protector, but I lodged there for nearly two years in the opening phases of the war.

When we arrived at Ashby we were received regally, the reception committee including doctors, auxiliary nurses in uniform and many local ladies. Obviously much work had been done in preparation for the event and billeting went without a hitch. For the whole of the School's stay we were treated most hospitably, and I almost became one of the natives. The boys and staff were billeted with local families, or stayed at the Manor House, a former resort of the aristocracy, or in a big house called St. Helens. Some of the staff were lodged in hotels.

Obviously the town had been somnolent until our arrival but we, the poor evacuees, woke it up to engender much gossip and astonishment. A colleague and I were billeted with a local bachelor bank-manager for the first few weeks. He was rather womanish in attitude and I fear that our robust city ways did not meet with his approval and he showed his resentment at the disruption of his social life, especially his bridge-playing parties, to which we were not invited. He employed a man-servant and wife, who kept a cat, and one night after my co-digger and I returned to our billet, having had a few beers, and our host having retired to bed, I threw the cat into his bedroom upstairs and the next thing I heard was his bedroom window being raised and the cat meowing on the lawn below.

We were asked to leave the next day and accommodated in the Queen's Hotel—we taught in the afternoon to alternate with the local grammar school's morning session. Gorgeous in those days were the evening meals in the Queen's of soup, ham and eggs and accompaniment and 'afters' provided by the landlady, Mrs. Tipton, and her son. She was a kind and generous woman, allowing soldiers serving in the area to take a free bath in the hotel—a true wartime spirit.

Some of the upper-crust were not so generous. One of our schoolboys residing with a factory owner in an extremely large house found on his return from school one evening his total belongings stacked in the hall and was given orders to leave. The boy's crime had been that he had not cleaned the bath after his morning ablutions. No account had been taken of the fact that the boy came from a poor home in Aston, Birmingham, where bathrooms were a rarity.

The most startling man in the town was one who refused point blank to billet evacuees, even though he lived in a large house with extensive grounds and employed two gardeners. The strange factor was that he had come from a working-class family and had been educated and nurtured at the expense of the South Wales Miners Federation, being its spokesman at one time, and had turned capitalist and snob. He also refused to act as Air Raid Warden or enrol in the Home Guard and got away with it. When he died, the caption in one of the national newspapers read 'The Light That Failed'. Maybe he had come to believe that colliers should know their place.

Some people certainly acted as if they should, which riled me as the son of an ex-miner. I remember a miner's agent, the manager and controller of three local coalmines visiting the Miners' Rescue Station at Ashby. It was staffed by experienced coalminers, and how surprised I was to see them touch their caps deferentially at his approach. To me it seemed like a relic of Feudalism. Incidentally, to be attached to the Rescue Station was a job fraught with danger. A neighbour and good friend of mine died down a mine from gas when called out on a rescue operation.

But to return to the lighter side of life at Ashby: in the afternoon the staff were peripatetic, making their way from base to base, teaching at the Manor House, at the rear of the Royal, in a small dance hall above a block of shops and called 'Gay Flats', or at 'St. Helens', the big town house. The last mentioned, like all boys' hostels, was the scene of an amusing episode. A boy was persuaded that he had a disease called tadpolitis, for into his bath water the boys had poured a jar of tadpoles. The victim was very gullible and reported his fear that he had a grave malady to the resident master-in-charge.

In between afternoon lessons to enable the staff to make their way from one base to the next was a twenty-minute break, and I sometimes called during an interval at the Hole In The Wall. There I met the local characters and heard the latest item of gossip. Gossip there was in plenty. It was reported to my headmaster that I drank a lot, but his magnanimous and commonsense reply was if it were so, it was because I could hold it. It would have taken a lot to intoxicate me in those days, for the beer was a wartime brew, a weak 10d. per pint beer, derisively called by the locals 'tenpenny' or 'tiger-spit'. How prices have risen in so short a time. Before the war beer was 4d. per pint, 5d. in the smoke room. Whisky was 12/6. per bottle, petrol 11½d. per gallon, matches ¼d. per box, best brand cigarettes 11½d. per twenty.

I have mentioned the fact that as in all small towns there was a lot of tattle and one rumour that spread around the town like wildfire was that a girl evacuee, a pupil of our co-lateral school, the King Edward Grammar School for Girls, had been made pregnant by one of the boys of my school. It could have been worse, there could have been an implication that it was one of the boys' staff. The staff in those early days had not been exempt from rumour. A report had circulated that two of my colleagues were in the habit of going to bed with their boots on, the cause being drunkenness. The irony was that one of them was a teetotaller. But I must have overcome my reputation for being bibulous, for when the School attended church service on Sundays, I was promoted to sidesman and took round the collection plate.

The tempo of war increased and I became resident in the Bull's Head. When air-raid sirens sounded mine-host and myself ensconced ourselves in the cellar, where he and I quaffed morale-boosting drinks until the all-clear siren sounded. I remember one such occasion when the German bombers zoomed frighteningly above before turning to dive on Coventry and saturate it with bombs. That was when the German propaganda machine chose to invent the word 'to Coventrate'. Only one bomb fell on Ashby, though, and I remember the horrible zooming noise it made as it descended, while my wife and I with our newly born son sheltered in the cellar of our house to which we had removed from the Bull's Head. I had married in 1940, my wife Kathleen being a schoolteacher from St. Helens.

By then the threat of invasion had resulted in the formation of the Home Guard and Air Raid Wardens. I was a member of the latter, and we were based in the biggest hotel in the town, being on duty on a rota system; duty meant being in attendance all night. To stay awake we kept making cups of tea, and as a diversion made bets for a small sum on the probable winner of cockroaches racing around. After my duty night I had to teach in the afternoon following a short sleep.

The Home Guard headquarters was in the belfry on top of the church adjacent to the castle. On one occasion one of the defenders, a town friend of mine, stunned himself by hitting his head against the lintel of the belfry, when he sprang up, gun in hand to defend the area—another of the Home Guard had inadvertently pulled a bell down below, the bell denoting an enemy invasion.

Happy days I spent amidst the local people, among whom characters stood out. There was Jackie Vann, resident at a local inn kept by his sister. He had been invalided out of the army at an early age and once every month travelled to Leicester in the morning, resplendent in morning dress, top hat and carnation, to claim his medical break-down pension. On his return in the afternoon he blew it all at his sister's hotel.

Probably the greatest character in the town was a barber with a reputation for being a great wit and practical joker. In devilment, in the local inns, he had the habit of cutting men's ties in half with a scissors. All taken in good part, for he always bought the victim a new tie afterwards. At night he used to terrify Charlie, the steward of one of the town's clubs, by chasing him around and prodding him with a billiard cue. Charlie had a pet goldfish, which disappeared one night, for one of the members took it home for his supper.

Happy days after my marriage, when I left the Bull's Head despite the fact that I was by no means wealthy. My teacher's salary was a pittance, less than £3 per week, and once I had to sell to a local collier the only gold watch I possessed to make both ends meet. Coal was expensive and on ration and often difficult to obtain. On more than one occasion the locals were surprised to see me, a schoolmaster, wheeling home through the streets in a barrow coke from the local gasworks. What fuel I got, I supplemented by walking down, at dead of night the railway line, which skirted the back of my garden, to a field where there had been chopped down trees to make a clearing. I returned laden with huge branches, which I threw over my garden wall to be chopped into firewood.

But to counter my lack of affluence was the fact that the cost of living was cheap and my wife, self and young son never went short of food. I was always one penny in hand and not in deficit, summed up by a Dickensian character as the difference between bliss and constant anxiety.

Though still resident at Ashby during the last year of the war I taught at Aston on Mondays and Tuesdays, since the school there had been re-opened for Birmingham-based boys. I taught at Ashby during the rest of the week. On the Monday I stayed the night at school, where I was on fire-watching duty. The occasional fire-bomb dropped on the playground only to be instantly smothered by 'Chaz' the School porter using sandbags. He was so cool, calm and methodical that my assistance was but rarely needed. One last Hudsonism is worth quoting. When a mother sought an interview with the Head, Chaz's reply was 'I'll see if he is vacant.'

The war came to an end, and on the night of VE Day and VJ Day the people of Ashby, myself included, celebrated in the main street. It was bedecked with flags hanging down from every house and we sang and cavorted round bonfires until early morning.

I dwelt in Ashby for a whole year after the end of the war, commuting to Aston daily. When I returned to Birmingham for good, I was given a right royal farewell by my Ashby friends. I give heartfelt thanks to the good people of Ashby for their wonderful hospitality to a poor evacuee.

I remained on the staff at King Edward School until the autumn of 1971, when I retired after forty-two years of teaching. I've learned a lot of things in my graduation to old age and none more important than to tolerate the foibles of fellow human beings and to spread as much happiness around as one can. The game of rugby has helped me learn that and I'm very grateful for it.

Index

Aarvold, Carl, 48-50, 54
Allen, J. W., 58, 62
Arthur, Tom, 54, 57, 75
Auckland, Jack, 17

Badger, Owen, 16
Bancroft, W. J., 34
Barbarians, 80-3
Bark-Jones, Raymond, 53
Barrington, Jim, 50-1
Bassett, Jack, 49-50, 52, 57-9, 61-4, 75, 77-8
Beattie, Jock, 57, 62
Bedford (England), 51
Bergh (S. Afr.), 78
Beynon, Harry, 29
Black, B. H., 51-2, 54
Boon, Ronnie, 50, 53, 55, 57, 59 61-2, 75, 77
Booth (England), 55
Bowcott, Harry, 53, 55, 57-8, 73
Bowdler, A. F., 49, 76
Bowen, D. Harry, 15-16
Bowker, J., 69, 84
Bowker, T., 72
Bradburn, Tommy, 70
Brand, G., 75, 77-8
Brown, Tom, 54
Buchanan, A., 15
Burland, Don, 52, 54

Calder, Ian, 72
Cardiff,
  Wales v. Ireland, 1932, 63-4
  v. Scotland, 1972, Photo facing, 33
  1931, 57-9

Championship,
  1931, 59
  1932, 63-4
  See also County Championship
Charlton (E. Midlands), 72
Chubb, J., 72
Clement, Will, 35
Clint, N., 66-7, 72
Cooper, J. A., 72
Cotton, R. D., 71
County Championship,
  Semifinal, 1933, 71
    Press comment on W. Thomas, 74
  Semifinal, 1934, 72-3
    Press comment on W. Thomas, 74
  Final, 1935, 84-6
    Press comment on W. Thomas, 86
Cove-Smith, R., 48
Cowley Grammar School, St. Helens, 39-42
Craven, A., 71, 86
Craven, Danny, 75-6, 78
Crichton-Miller (Scotland), 57-8

Daneel (S. Afr.) 75, 78
Daniels, D. J., 16
Davey, Claude, 35-6, 50, 52-5, 57-8, 72, 75, 77
Davies, Ben, 16
Davies, H. Graham, 18
Davies, Trevor, 35
Davies, Will, 35, 75-7
Day, Tom, 36, 50, 58, 76

East Midlands,
   v. Lancashire, 1933, 71
     1934, 72-3
Edmunds, Dick, 18
Elliot, Wally, 54-5
v. England (Twickenham),
   1927, 46-8
   1929, 48-50
   1931, 50-2
   1933, 53-6
Estcourt, E. S., 72
Evans, Bobbie, 18-19
Evans, Bryn, 18, 53
Evans, Frank, 18-19
Evans, Tom, 17
Evans, Tosh, 22

Fender, Norman, 50, 57
Foulds, Roy, 48
Fry, H. C. (Harry), 72, 74, 84-5

Gabe, Rhys T., 17
Gadney, B. C., 72-3
Gordon, Frank 'Genny', 34
Gore, Eric, 72
Guest, R. (Dickie), 67-70, 72

Harding, Rowe, 35
Hay, Sid, 32
Heaton, Jack, 69-70, 72, 80, 84, 86
Hiddlestone, Dai, 18-19
Horne, F. B. R., 71
Hopkins, Morgan, 83
Howard, P. D., 51
Howells, John, 16
Hughes, D. T. Glynn, 80

Inverleith, 60
Ireland at Cardiff, 1932, 63-4
Isaacs, Iorrie, 54

Jenkins, Albert, 15, 18, 20
Jenkins, D. R., 35
Jenkins, Ned, 33, 57, 75
Jenkins, Vivien, 53, 55
John, Barry, 20
John, Dai, 32-3
John, J. H., 35

Jones, Dai, 48
Jones, Edgar, 53
Jones, Ivor, 49
Jones, R., 49
Jones, Tom, 60
Jones, Vaughan, 53
Jones-Davies, T. E., 50-1

King Edward VI Grammar School,
   Aston, 87-90

Laird, Colin, 48, 50
Lancashire, 69-74, 84-6
   County Champions, 1935, 83-5
    Photo facing, 72
   v. E. Midlands, 1934, 72-3
   v. Somerset, 1935, 84-6
    Press comment on W. Thomas,
    86
Lancashire & Cheshire
   v. Springboks, 1931 (incl. press
    comment on W. Thomas), 79
Leather, W. H., 72
Lemon, Arthur, 50, 57, 75, 77
Leyland, Roy, 69, 72, 80, 84
Lightfoot (Ireland), 63
Lind, Harry, 57-8, 62
Llanelli County (Grammar)
   School, 25-7
Llanelli RFC,
   v. Aberavon (away), 1934, 32-3
   v. Australia, 1908, 17
   v. Maoris, 1881, 15-16
   v. Maoris, 1926, 32
    Photo facing, 32
   v. Newport, 1926, 31
   v. South Africa, 1906, 17
Llanelli RFC supporters, 21-2
Llewellyn, Willie, 17, 57
Longland, Ray, 54, 73
Louw, 'Boy', 75

McArthur, J. B., 72
McCanlis (Gloucester), 50
McPherson (Scotland), 57-8
Male, Ossie, 48

Manley, D. P., 35
Margrave, Fred, 15
Matthews, A. D., 73
Meikle, G. S. C., 72
Meikle, G. W. C., 72
Morgan, Ivor, 18, 34
Morgan, Teddy, 57
Morley, J. C. (Jack), 50, 52, 57-8,
    62-3, 75, 77-8
Morris, Bill, 16
Mostert, Phil, 75
Murrayfield, 1932, 59-63
Mycock, Joe, 72, 74, 84-5

Ogden, 'Pop', 70
Osler, Benny, 33, 75-6, 78

Palmer, Bert, 34
Pank, J. C., 72, 84
Parker, Dai, 35
Powell, W. C., 49-51, 57-8, 62-3
Press comments on W. Thomas, 74,
    79, 86
Price, H. L., 46

Ralph, A. R., 62-4, 75
Rees, Walter, 36
Roderick, Buckley, 15
Rogers, John D., 15
Roncoroni, Tony, 54
Roughhead, Mick, 57-8, 62
Rugby League, 43-5

St. Helens RFC, 43
St. Helens Recreation, 43
  v. Scotland, 1931 (Cardiff), 57-9
    1932 (Murrayfield), 59-63
Seaside Stars RFC, 16-17
Sissa, Emile de, 80
Skym, Archie, 50, 53, 57, 75-6
Slow (E. Midlands), 72-3
Smeddle, R. W., 48
Smith, Haigh, 80
Smith, Ian, 57, 60, 62
Somerset v. Lancashire, 1935, 83-5
Springboks v. Lancs & Cheshire
    (incl. press comment on W.
    Thomas), 79

v. Wales, 1931 (Swansea), 75-9
Stacey, A. J., 17-18
Stoop, A. D., 46
Stott, Eddie, 70
Swansea,
    Wales v. Springboks, 1931, 75-9
Swansea RFC, 33-8
    French tour, 1928-9, 37-8
Swansea University RFC, 29

Tallant, J. E., 73
Thomas, Dai, 54
Toft, H. B. (Bert), 70, 72, 84-5
Treen (E. Midlands), 72
Trew, W. J., 34
Trew, W. J., Junior, 35
Tucker, Sam, 48, 51
Turnbull, Maurice, 53
Twickenham 1927, 46-8
    1929, 48-50
    1931, 50-2
    1933, 53-6
    1933, Photo facing, 65

Vallance, G. P. C., 71-2

Wales
    Champions, 1931, 59
    v. England (at Twickenham),
        1927, 46-8
        1929, 48-50
        1931, 50-2
        1933, 53-6
        1933, Photo facing, 65
    v. Ireland, 1932 (Cardiff), 63-4
    v. Scotland, 1927 (Cardiff),
        Photo facing, 33
        1931 (Cardiff), 57-9
        1932 (Murrayfield), 59-63
    v. South Africa, 1931 (Swansea),
        75-9
Waterloo RFC, 65-8
Waters, F. H., 62
Watkins, Elwyn, 35
Watkins, Harry, 16
Webb, Charlie, 54
Welsh, W. B., 57, 62
Wemyss, Jock, 61, 80

Whelpton, G. W., 72
Whitfield, Jack, 60
White, Joe, 36
Wilkinson, H., 48-50

Williams, Frank, 75
Wilson (England), 50
Wood (Scotland), 58
Wooler, Wilfred, 53-5